"The digital world is growing in its impact on our families. Parents become overwhelmed and anxious about how to raise their kids in healthy ways when they are constantly faced with their kids' engagement in more and more screen time. They don't know how much of a battle to have, or even if they should have one. Stephen Arterburn and Alice Benton provide a practical, biblically based, and research-proven approach that will guide you through the questions and issues that will come up. You'll be empowered with great tools to navigate these waters. Highly recommended."

—**John Townsend,** psychologist, author of the bestselling *Boundaries* series, and founder of the Townsend Institute and Townsend Leadership Group

"A few words I would use to describe *Understanding and Loving Your Child in a Screen-Saturated World* would be empowering, practical, and actionable. Parenting is difficult enough as it is, and trying to fight children over their amount of screen time is frustrating and never-ending. This book brings grace into your daily life in a realistic way and enables you to build a relationship with your children through positive interactions using screens. Instead of fighting over the use of screens, this book shows you how to give yourself and your family grace. Each chapter is full of examples from daily life, tips, and questions on how to put the information you have learned into practice. As I read this book, I was so excited to be able to recommend it to parents in this age of screen saturation. I love the honesty of the authors and the situations presented in each chapter. This book gives a positive spin on something most parents feel is a negative in their child's life and helps parents work with technology instead of against it."

—**Bonnie Worthen,** director of children's ministry at First Christian Church of Huntington Beach

"I'm frequently asked to review manuscripts for publication, and I must admit, I'm very picky about my choices. When Dr. Benton asked me to review her work, I was delighted to accept because I personally know of her integrity and desire to become a better wife and mother. This book blew me away, and I learned so much. Her research on the topic of screen time is exceptional, and her blend with Christianity shows a roundedness not often seen in works like this. I have four adult sons and daughters and ten grandchildren. I will be buying this book for all of them and everyone else I know with children and teens. I enthusiastically endorse this great contribution to a critical topic that is threatening the relationships within our culture."

—**Rev. Milan Yerkovich,** president of Milan & Kay Resources, founder of Relationship180 Counseling Center, co-host and teacher at New Life Ministries, and coauthor of *How We Love* and *How We Love Our Kids*

"This is a must-read for any parent who desires to raise healthy children in this digital world. I have learned to shift from a Limiter to a Mentor and am seeing the benefit of teaching our children how to engage with media in a safe, healthy way. Instead of saying no to things based out of fear, I engage with our children to learn and research together what may be appropriate and what may be harmful...and sometimes it's the kids setting their OWN boundaries! This book has been a blessing to our family!"

—**Chelsee Jensen,** mother of teenagers

Understanding and Loving Your Child in a Screen-Saturated World

UNDERSTANDING
AND LOVING
YOUR CHILD
IN A SCREEN-SATURATED WORLD

STEPHEN ARTERBURN
and ALICE BENTON

SALEM
BOOKS
an imprint of Regnery Publishing
Washington, D.C.

The authors are represented by the literary agency of WordServe Literary (www. wordserveliterary.com).

ISBN: 978-1-68451-157-0
eISBN: 978-1-68451-440-3

Published in the United States by
Salem Books
An Imprint of Regnery Publishing
A Division of Salem Media Group
Washington, D.C.
www.SalemBooks.com

Manufactured in the United States of America

10 9 8 7 6 5 4 3 2 1

Books are available in quantity for promotional or premium use. For information on discounts and terms, please visit our website: www.SalemBooks.com

CONTENTS

CONTENTS

Confessions of an Ignorant Parent

by Stephen Arterburn

"Thinking myself to be wise, I, Stephen, instead became an utter fool." This is my painful paraphrase of Romans 1:22 that perfectly describes me before my eyes were opened to the extreme evil and dark corners of the internet, social media, and all aspects of the world behind the screens our kids are glued to. I thought I knew what a contentious parent needed to know about all things online, but in 2003, I was concerned for my thirteen-year-old daughter and other children who were being bullied and exposed to information and images that no one of any age should experience or see. I read anything and everything I could find to equip myself to protect my daughter and her future. With all my newly absorbed knowledge and presumed wisdom, I set out to write a book to equip, inspire, and motivate parents to do all they could do to fight a rising tide of darkness infiltrating almost every home in America. So in 2007, I coauthored and published a book titled *Internet Protect Your Kids* with Roger Marsh.

Back then, parents told us it was helpful, but that book would not provide enough information and insight for parents today who want to protect their children from the severe damage that screens can incur. That book devoted an entire section to discussing MySpace. MySpace no longer exists, but there is still a dark web that is designed to feed our children the sickest of images and connect them to the most evil information, beliefs, connections, and experiences. And adults as well.

One of my children was introduced to the dark web at the age of eight while visiting a friend whose parents I admired. They were unaware that a neighbor had shown their child how to access the dark web.

Together, our two young children watched a video of terrorists forcing a man to his knees and beheading him with one slash of a long sword—then using his severed head as a soccer ball.

I foolishly thought I knew what was going on with my kids, that they shared with me their struggles and challenges—but they did not. In this case, it was so traumatic that I didn't learn about it until a year later. I thought the internet filters we put in place were enough—but they never will be as long as kids are left unattended with devices that open them up to the most evil content.

The internet is like so many other things: it has great potential for good, while at the same time it can be used for extremely unhealthy and destructive purposes. Pornography had already become the biggest online industry in 2007, and it quickly trapped some good people into some really bad habits that destroyed lives, marriages, and families. And the internet's power has only grown since then.

Today, we live in an entirely different reality that neither Roger nor I saw coming when we wrote our book. The internet and social media have created a screen-saturated world that directly opposes traditional values and biblical standards for morality. That's why I asked my friend, Dr. Alice Benton, to cowrite this book with me. She has been one of our favorite co-hosts on our broadcast, *New Life Live*, due to her rare combination of a bright mind and big heart for those who struggle with life's toughest challenges. I wanted her to bring that combination to this book; she did that and more. Dr. Benton is deeply spiritual and committed to both her children and yours. She has exceeded expectations in developing the most helpful insights and strategies to combat the greatest threat to the souls of our children: the society behind the screens.

CHAPTER 1

Are Your Children Getting Enough Screen Time with You?

I f we lived in a cocaine-saturated world, we would all be at
high risk of becoming cocaine users and addicts. And the
first necessary step to solve the problem would be to throw
away all the cocaine. Thank God we don't live in a cocaine-
saturated world. We do, however, live in a screen-saturated
world, and we are all susceptible to developing problematic
and even addictive screen use, but tossing out all the screens,
or even severely limiting their use, is actually not the solution.
Approximately one in four people (adults and youth) meet the
diagnostic criteria for screen addiction.[1] Most of us know that
we ourselves are overly attached to our smartphones, and we
are rightfully worried about our children's digital pursuits. But
the solution is not to primarily limit our children's access to

screens, as I once believed. The complex antidote to our susceptibility to screen addiction might surprise you—especially the fact that purposefully increasing screen time *as a family* can actually decrease the risk of developing a personal screen addiction. I'll explain how and why.

Vulnerability to any type of addiction increases when one is isolated, lonely, and unhappy, and screen addiction is no exception. Other risk factors include high-conflict homes, harsh parenting, and lack of supervision.[2] Protective factors include humbly imperfect parents, ramping up communal family screen time, digital mentoring, relational comfort, high parental expectations, and involvement in faith practices. We can begin today to build a hedge of protection around our families by constructing better relationships and playfully relating with our children both onscreen and offscreen.

Together we will learn how to implement research-based, biblically supported, personally tested strategies to safeguard our households from addiction or to treat it if it has already taken hold. A full-on frontal attack of our children's digital behavior is not an effective technique. You've probably tried that and found yourself facing a child with heels dug in, hands tightly gripping his smartphone. So breathe a sigh of relief, because there is a more effective approach. We will focus on employing relationship-enhancing techniques to help the entire family develop emotional awareness and regulation as well as to decrease parent-child conflict. We will learn to apply motivational strategies to increase long-lasting, genuine self-esteem through task mastery and self-control. This approach will naturally help loosen screens' unhealthy grip on our families. These positive activities will increase our children's buy-in to this philosophy and reduce resistant rebellion. Together, we will augment digital blessings and decrease digital damage. You and your children will experience change. Throughout, I will share with you how I've practiced these principles with my own family. Admittedly, the ideas contained herein are simple to understand and yet challenging to consistently apply. But together, we can take authority over our screens and use them for good.

If you had told me three years ago that I would one day advocate for an increase in my children's screen time and a decrease in my own, I would have said you were nuts. I admire homes that don't even have a television. A "screen-free home" sounds quite virtuous to my ears. Perhaps you have an aversion to screen time for your children as well, and you wonder if the best approach is to limit it as much as possible.

It could be that you love digital technology and are delighted with how savvy your children are with their screens. Maybe you are a skilled gamer and relish getting in a few hours of

Madden, Minecraft, or *Fortnite* with your children. Perhaps you fall somewhere in between and wonder how much to encourage and how much to limit their usage. This book is for all of us who want to equip our children for the real world. Join me on what has become an unexpected personal journey. Together, we will wade through the most recent research, learn to apply the most effective psychological strategies, and invite God and His principles to guide us as we work to understand how to love our children in this screen-saturated world.

•   •   •

I grew up in a conservative Midwestern Catholic home in the 1980s. The lone television, kept in my parents' bedroom, was rarely on. My mom took a very protective stance against television, believing it to be a subpar use of time. The single exception was watching one or two movies, which she would choose, when my parents were out on a date on Friday nights. The movie choices were restricted mainly to those starring Fred Astaire and Ginger Rogers or John Wayne, and a few pre-recorded cartoons. That was about it. We watched only with explicit permission on each occasion.

My parents rarely turned on the television for themselves. My pappa worked long hours running an auto repair shop. He did not watch news or sports on TV. My mom played conservative talk radio through most of the day as her source of news and entertainment. We never owned a video game console. My mom had a work computer and occasionally allowed us to play *Oregon Trail* and *Where in the World Is Carmen Sandiego?* To her credit and foresight, she enrolled us all in several computer classes in grade school to learn about typing, the internet, emails, and chat rooms.

Two of my siblings have continued to live out the philosophy that digital activity is not an ideal way for kids to spend their time. Neither of them even has a television in their home. They watch some movies on the computer occasionally on the weekends or when the kids are sick. I'll admit, I admire them and have felt that I don't measure up to the family standard.

My husband grew up in California in a family with a more relaxed attitude toward screens. His family enjoyed and found benefit in regularly having the TV on for news and entertainment. It is comfortable for him to have the television on in the background, usually with football or a golf tournament playing. He loves watching sports, movies, news, and nature shows.

As an adult, I've never been terribly drawn to watch much television. I'm a reader, and I find that books generally hold my interest and are more enjoyable than shows. My prideful workaholism has historically compelled me to pursue chronic productivity, which has limited my ability to relax with my family.

You can imagine that my husband and I have had many a challenge in figuring out how to balance our sometimes-opposing views. My self-righteous certainty that my philosophy is holier has added to the tension.

Just to prove how digitally pure my life was as I began my research for this book, I installed a monitoring app called StayFree, which shows me how much I use each system on my phone. After using it for several weeks, I was stunned to see that I unlocked my phone an average of thirty-nine times per day. (Sixty-eight unlocks in one day is my current record.) I use my phone for up to five hours each day. Folks, those numbers really took me aback. How many of those minutes spent glued to my phone led my children to think I check it too often and that they are less important to me? And yet, in my hypocrisy and blindness, I was only limiting *their* digital activity. I thought I limited my own well enough. But those numbers on my monitoring app don't lie.

Digital technology allows me to work from home and enriches my life in many ways. And yet I have felt maniacally driven to limit my children's access to it. I have been very protective, with a tendency to be extremely restrictive of their digital activity. I have barely been able to tolerate their digital exposure. I would rarely—if ever—choose to participate in it with them! I don't want to watch cartoons. I don't want to play video games. And frankly, I don't want to let them do these things either. We probably wouldn't have a television in our home if it weren't for my husband's more balanced view of the world.

Before writing this book, I spent the majority of my days attached to a screen with little to no awareness of my hypocrisy. I kept my phone on my bedside table at night, and it served as my alarm clock in the morning and my watch throughout the day. (I'm on a screen during my workday, providing remote therapy by telephone and videoconference to clients across the country.) Between sessions, I would usually scroll through social media as my "breather."

As soon as my work was done for the day, I would shut down my computer. However, I kept my phone near me through the evening to respond to work and personal alerts, often checking it while in conversation with my children. I fully sanctioned my own level of screen use.

Hypocritically, whenever I found my kiddos in front of a screen, my stomach would twist into a knot of protest. *Screens aren't good for my children!* And no matter how tired I was, I would insist on turning their screen off, usually without warning. I would internally criticize my husband for turning the screen on for them, but he could always feel the tension of my unspoken rebuke. Then I would pat myself on the back for being so diligent about turning the screen off.

My screen use would continue once the kids were in bed, as my husband and I enjoyed catching an episode of *Maine Cabin Masters* or *Life Below Zero*. If I was lucky, I could keep my eyes open long enough to snatch fifteen minutes more at the end of the night reading a book in bed through Kindle.

Unbeknownst to me, I needed a digital attitude adjustment. I had allowed my screens to dominate my own life to a detrimental degree. My fear and judgment of my family's screen time had practically blinded me to the potential fun, education, relational power, engagement, and life enhancement possible through digital activities. And my judgmental attitude was weighing heavily on my husband and children.

The information that follows caused me to reconsider and adjust my entire philosophy.

•   •   •

Through surveys of thousands of families over a two-year period, Dr. Alexandra Samuel, a data journalist with a doctorate in political science, identified three patterns of digital parenting styles and their consequences. She discovered that parents tend to be Limiters, Enablers, or Mentors.[3]

Limiter parents are apprehensive about the ways screen time can potentially harm their children: impaired attention span; stunted social development; and physical, mental, and psychological side effects. Limiters probably grew up with a low level of screen time. They believe that activities such as outdoor play, reading, and pursuing non-screen hobbies are *always* better than digital activity. Boy, does that describe me in a nutshell.

Enabler parents allow their children to hold the digital decision-making power, deferring to their children's knowledge and preferences for their online use. Enablers have a relaxed attitude about devices and believe that most digital behavior, whether structured or not, is beneficial for their children. Enablers believe that attempts to restrict digital activity will result in excessive, unhelpful drama.[4]

Mentor parents purposefully and frequently bring their children online to teach and guide while keeping structure and high standards. Mentors have boundaries around their own screen time. They are more likely to disconnect from their own digital pursuits in order to interact with their children. They allow their children to have opinions that influence family screen agreements. These parents tend to have expectations about limiting screen use during mealtimes and at bedtime. Mentors frequently speak about online behavior, teach their children online etiquette, and enroll them in classes and workshops to enhance their digital knowledge. Mentors research new digital devices, apps, and activities for their children. Mentors regularly play video games with their kids. (My jaw dropped when I first read that information.)

Dr. Samuel found that the children of Limiters (like my children) are *the most likely to access pornography accidentally or intentionally*, and to be rude and hostile online. Children of Limiters are three times as likely to impersonate a parent or peer online! To my surprise, children of Enablers are at lower risk for these behaviors than children of Limiters. However, children of Enablers are at the highest risk for communicating and exchanging information with strangers online. The children of Mentor parents are the most likely to have the healthiest digital behavior in the long run.

No matter how much we restrict screens when our children are young, they will soon have access that we will not be able to control. Unlike my childhood, today 94 percent of American kids fifteen years and older have a smartphone.[5] If we never turn the screens on at all, or turn them off every chance we get, our children will be unprepared for the real world as it is today and will be more likely to engage in risky digital behavior when they do get their hands on a screen. On the other end of the spectrum, if we allow our children to run their own digital life, they are likely to be victimized by online predators.

There is a healthier middle road.

If you haven't been a Mentor either, we are both missing out on the chance to know, protect, minister to, and love on our children in this digital age. Dr. Samuel recommends six steps parents can take to become better Mentors.[6]

1. **Model for your children the digital behavior you want them to emulate.** I propose implementing what I call the 4T Challenge. The 4T's stand for Talking, Table, Traffic, and Toilet. In other words, work to eliminate screen use while Talking face-to-face with someone else, while eating at the dinner Table (or keeping them on your bedside Table), while driving in Traffic, or while using the Toilet. It works best for parents to implement these strategies first, and after achieving some success, have your children join in the challenge. In order to personally master these areas, I had to

buy an old-fashioned wristwatch, an alarm clock, and good ol' paperback books to replace my utilitarian smartphone. I also had to set up accountability with friends. It was hard! But I can now hold these standards for my children with a clear conscience.

2. **Encourage your children to develop their digital skills. You might research and introduce them to new educational apps.** Rather than constantly turning screens off, I now intentionally invite my children to use apps that meet our family values. I also occasionally invite my children to play video games with me (although this is still outside my comfort zone). This has dramatically decreased the tension in our home and increased our level of playfulness and joy. I also have a stronger sense of authority and influence, rather than feeling the out-of-control anxiety I used to experience around my children's screen time. My husband and our kids greatly appreciate the change in my approach.

3. **Include your children in developing family agreements for digital use rather than imposing unilateral parental rules.** One way we do this is to allow our children to choose which chores they will

complete in order to earn their digital activity and to choose how long they will use the screen. We give them several options from which to choose.

4. **Monitor how different digital activities affect your children's emotions.** Particular forms of digital engagement can lead to children becoming hyperactive, overwhelmed, fearful, or depressed. For example, we chose to limit car-racing video games for a time because our son would almost always become anxious, tearful, and have tantrums when he would play.

5. **Be mindful of how you handle your children's privacy online.** I never thought to ask my children's permission to post photos or videos of them online—but they have their own preferences, which tend to change with age. Our youngest, Walter, did not want his face online. I was shocked that he had an opinion about it at all and was glad that I asked.

6. **Talk with your children about their digital activity.** In my ignorance and impatience, I had little to no desire to talk about my children's digital interests, which can leave them feeling unimportant and overlooked. And if we are ignorant of

their online pursuits, we are probably leaving them unprotected.

I now believe that I should be participating in and encouraging my family's digital pursuits rather than focusing so heavily on fearful restriction. Therefore, I have been working to transform my approach—but honestly, it still isn't easy for me to do.

Despite my obsession with the off button on the remote, I do want my children to see technology as a blessing and a potential enhancer of life. I want to model and teach them to use it appropriately and with self-control. I know that you want the same for your children. Join me in applying these six techniques in order to become better digital Mentors.

CHAPTER 2

Comfort

The digital realm is a convenient source of comfort, easy access to friends, entertainment, and distraction. In our high-paced, stressful world, we use a variety of coping tools to deal with our emotional distress. When we feel overwhelmed, taking a real-world break in the digital domain can soothe us just enough to be able to return to messy reality. Distraction is a powerful coping tool—and it can be a healthy one, especially when used in moderation and balanced with other means of coping. Mentor parents are keyed in to the types of digital activities that are soothing to themselves and their children. More importantly, they use them appropriately.

Every day, we are confronted with any number of frustrations, hurts, and challenges. Our emotions are stirred up within us. If we do not address and deal with them, they accumulate, and this is detrimental in the long run. I liken it to a can of soda (or as we Midwesterners call it, "pop"). Charged emotional events online and offline shake up our internal can of soda. We can handle it for a while and keep a lid on it. But eventually, we'll reach the tipping point when a seemingly small frustration pops the top and a messy explosion of emotional soda sprays all over the place.

One day, practically everything seemed to go awry with my children. If it could spill, it did. If it could break, it did. All three kiddos were whining and complaining much more than they normally do for most of the day. Alerts continuously sounded from my phone with requests from clients and updates from friends. Any attempt I made to address the online activity was interrupted by surround-sound clamoring from my children.

I had started off the morning with energy and patience, but each new annoyance ate away at my waning internal resources. By the end of the day, it was a kicky diaper change that did me in. Who knew that a toddler's foot to the gut could be that painful? What would normally be a doable task became an unexpected trigger for an elevated voice, edgy tone, and angry face from me. We were all tense, frustrated, and on each other's nerves by that point. What had happened? Our emotional soda cans had been shaken up all day. The requirements of the day depleted our resources, and that last diaper strike popped my top.

So when I gave my children permission to watch a cartoon and I took a few minutes to scroll through my social media, the emotional temperature in the room quickly dropped several degrees. We all calmed down and were better able to manage the rest of the evening without lashing out and sniping at each other. This screen break worked as a stop-gap measure for the simmering frustration and fatigue. Screen distraction can be a quick superficial fix, as other forms of distraction or resolution may require more parental energy and patience than is accessible on an empty tank. Distraction should be a temporary solution that can hold us until deeper resolution can take place.

Many folks report feeling better when engaging with digital media. After a stressful situation, it has become a habit for me to scroll through Facebook for a few minutes for a much-needed mental break. It feels soothing to me. How do you cope when your frustrations are mounting?

We each must determine the level at which digital distraction is helpful, when it reaches a point of diminishing returns, and when it becomes detrimental. This differs from one individual to the next.

Distraction can be an effective temporary fix for frustration from time to time. But what if this becomes our family's habitual response to stress and uncomfortable emotions? The kids are misbehaving: turn on the screen. My spouse and I are in conflict: turn on the screen. I'm overwhelmed by our bills and debt: turn on the screen. I'm anxious and feel socially inept and awkward: turn on the screen. If that's what I did, I would be teaching my children that the best method to address emotional disturbance is by turning on the screen. When we do that, a temporarily beneficial source of relief becomes the only method of coping, and the real problems go untreated.

Parents whose infants and toddlers are fussy and difficult to soothe tend to allow more media time.[1] When overwhelmed, many parents also turn to their own screens for relief from their children's emotional and behavioral problems. When families are chronically soothed with screen time, a vicious cycle begins to play out.[2] The children are temporarily pacified but then have greater difficulty regulating their emotions and behavior over time.[3] Children also tend to act out more as their parents become increasingly digitally disengaged. This increase in the misbehavior is in part a bid for their parents' attention.

The digital fix has neurochemical effects. Children who use three or more hours of entertainment media daily have unhealthy levels of the stress hormone cortisol.[4] Adolescents with higher levels of cell phone use, media exposure, and large numbers of friends on social networking sites also have higher levels of cortisol.[5] Such large numbers of digital relational connections may be greater than what is realistically manageable on an emotional, cognitive, and social level, thereby increasing rather than decreasing stress over time.

Perpetual digital distraction short circuits and bypasses the necessary deeper-level emotional resolution process. Distraction can become a digital bandage that covers and hides unresolved, festering emotions and higher levels of stress hormones. Mental health providers are seeing an increase in children who escape to their digital worlds to such an extent that they withdraw from the real world, which they feel ill-equipped to face. Using social media as the primary method to cope with stress can actually inhibit the body's ability to metabolize the higher levels of cortisol.[6]

According to a survey of 314 middle and high school students conducted in 2014 that was published in the *Journal of Black Studies*, 24 percent said they felt like they are "nothing" without their phones. Half indicated that they couldn't do without their phones for even a single day.[7] Many people reveal that they choose text-based conversations over face-to-face interactions because they are less stressful and messy. As digital interactions become the preferred form of communication, people report feeling more isolated, judged, and distressed.[8] Over time, their confidence atrophies and in-person social skills and emotional regulation get rusty.

In the long run, we are doing ourselves a disservice if we regularly choose the quicker fix and the easier way of doing life in order to avoid discomfort. The relief provided by digital pursuits can have an ugly underbelly. Excessive social networking is correlated with loneliness, worry, depression, and narcissistic behavior.[9] Many social media users report experiencing FOMO, the "Fear of Missing Out." It is a mixture of feeling excluded, anxious, and even rejected when seeing others' activities posted online. It can lead to unhealthy behaviors such as excessive checking of social media accounts and obsessing about the events one is not attending.[10]

A questionnaire has been developed to assess FOMO. It has been used in several research studies since its development and has been validated as an effective scale.[11]

Fear of Missing Out Scale					
Przybylski, Murayama, DeHaan, and Gladwell (2013) [12]					
1	2	3	4	5	
Completely False	Slightly True	Moderately True	Very True	Extremely True	Rating

1. I fear others have more rewarding experiences than me.

2. I fear my friends have more rewarding experiences than me.

3. I get worried when I find out my friends are having fun without me.

4. I get anxious when I don't know what my friends are up to.

5. It is important that I understand my friends' "in" jokes.

6. Sometimes, I wonder if I spend too much time keeping up with what is going on.

7. It bothers me when I miss an opportunity to meet up with friends.

8. When I have a good time, it is important for me to share the details online (e.g. updating my status).

9. When I miss out on a planned get-together, it bothers me.

10. When I go on vacation, I continue to keep tabs on what my friends are doing.

Total

The lowest score possible is ten, indicating an absence of FOMO. The highest possible score is fifty, indicating significant FOMO. Invite your children to take the questionnaire. Be gently curious about their answers while withholding your criticism.

The emotional struggle of feeling left out certainly existed before smartphones, but our digital age has significantly exacerbated it. When we see the second-by-second updates and photos of the parties, meals, and conversations that are taking place without us, we can all feel the sting of not being included. This can send us into a tailspin of wondering: *What's wrong with me? Why don't they like me? Am I out of the group? What did I say? What did I do wrong?* Most adults can identify pivotal events of exclusion that significantly impacted them years ago, sometimes all the way back to childhood. The hurtful effects can linger for years or even decades, especially if we repress, ignore, and divert our attention from the emotional pain.

Distressing emotions do not go away on their own, nor are they resolved through more digital distraction. They are, however, temporarily pacified through digital distraction. We must be cautious not to be fooled by the reprieve.

Let's take a deeper look at how emotions work, how they don't work, and the roles that distraction, comfort,

and resolution must play in order to have a healthy digital/
emotional life balance.

When faced with a perceived threat, the body is designed
to kick into gear to handle it. An internal process occurs in
which the sympathetic nervous system, which activates the
body to react to problems, manages two hormones, adrenaline
and cortisol, which are automatically released into the blood-
stream. In the short term, this process is beneficial and helps
us to address the threat by honing the body's functioning into
fight-or-flight mode. This is terrific when facing a woolly
mammoth. But what if today's woolly mammoth is the evasive
popularity contest that can't be won through a spear fight or
running away?

In cases of chronic stress and repressed emotions, the body
can essentially get stuck in fight-or-flight mode. Prolonged
stress responses are accompanied by elevated levels of adrenaline and cortisol, leading to a host of problems including anxiety, depression, weight gain, impaired sleep, digestive problems,
a compromised immune system, and even heart disease. This
concerning aftermath is likely to occur for anyone who goes
through the trials of life without true stress relief, particularly when those present-day trials ping an alert on the device
attached to one's body day and night. (Anyone else love and
hate their phone's alert?)

Although it feels like an enjoyable diversion to frequently turn on a screen, it also inundates the brain with what is generally an overwhelming amount of information—in many cases negative, distressing information. As has always been the case, most news media subscribe to the motto: "If it bleeds, it leads." Distressing news about events great and minor, over which we have no control, is always only a click away. Social media places us in a position of unavoidable comparison that can result in either unhealthy pride or feelings of inadequacy. Either we puff up narcissistically, reveling in the ways we are better than others, or we beat ourselves up as our flaws are pitted against others' filtered beauty. This comparison overload can leave us thinking, *Everyone I know looks better, thinner, stronger, and sexier than me. Their kids are more fun, they eat more eye-catching food, and they go on better adventures than we do. My life stinks in comparison.*

Uncomfortable though they may be, emotions give us vital information about our safety, needs, hurts, and how our interactions with others and the world affect us. Unpleasant emotions are usually warning signals trying to draw our attention to an unresolved issue. But it is difficult for us to tolerate the discomfort long enough to discover the need beneath the emotion and take action to resolve it. The more we distract, repress, and ignore our feelings, the more the unpleasantness accumulates below the surface. The emotional warning signal is not turned off by distraction. It is merely temporarily pushed from conscious awareness. Unresolved emotions and their connected issues always come back to the forefront, usually in disruptive ways. The ability to manage and resolve emotions comes with a steep learning curve, but it effectively equips a person to engage with the world successfully. Steve Arterburn first taught me this lesson through his book *Healing Is a Choice*.

So how can we enjoy the benefits, positive distractions, and healthy entertainment while protecting against the downside of digital activity and social media? We should balance our digital distraction by regularly accessing face-to-face relational comfort, and when that is not available, turning to non-digital self-soothing, such as exercise and reading. God-designed relational comfort returns cortisol to its rightful place, increases feel-good hormones such as oxytocin and dopamine, strengthens the relationships between parents and children, and builds character.

To progress toward overall healthy functioning, we must develop the courage, strength, and tools to embrace our own and our children's messy emotions. We must face these emotions head on, and both model and teach our children to "feel and deal." If we can patiently explore the reasons for our emotions, we are more likely to successfully resolve them. Emotional distress may appear to be random or illogical, but if sufficiently examined, there is always a reason and a root. The process of analysis teaches our children how to identify and manage their own needs. It is called Emotional Intelligence, and it is related to greater success in life.

Emotion	Potential Meaning
Anger	• Need to act: fight, protect, assert • Need to grieve (often hiding under the cover of anger) • Need to forgive • Need to establish or strengthen boundaries
Sadness	• Need to grieve • Need for comfort • Need to identify and express anger
Anxiety/Fear	• Need to release control • Need for comfort • Need for brainstorming/advice • Need to protect limited resources • Need to be protected
Guilt/Regret	• Need to confess • Need to be forgiven • Need to repair and reconcile

Emotion	Potential Meaning
Jealousy	• Need to experience disappointment • Need to grieve what is lacking • Need action to attend to/change the deficit • Need to confess covetousness
Joy	• Need to celebrate • Need to express gratitude

The Comfort Circle is the simplest, most effective process I know to address emotional distress. It was developed by Milan and Kay Yerkovich in their 2006 book, *How We Love*. It is a process of active listening through a set of steps designed to draw out, validate, and resolve emotions. Learning to use it has transformed my professional work, my marriage, and my parenting. If we parents learn to practice it frequently for ourselves and with our children, we will all become better equipped to regulate our emotions without having to escape into a screen every time we are upset.

How does this work? For example, when I am distressed, I ask my husband to follow this format in listening to me. When my children are upset, I use this process to be their listener. I use the Comfort Circle every day in sessions with my clients. The emotional relief this structured listening can produce is incredible and helps us to avoid turning to digital escape and distraction as a primary method of self-soothing. Here is a modified version:

Reflect:

1. Either identify together the problem or situation you need to discuss, or ask: Would you please tell me about something that is bothering you?
2. After listening, respond with: I heard you say

   _____

   (repeat their words **without adding your opinion**).
3. Did I understand you? Is what I said correct?
4. Would you please tell me more?

(Repeat Steps 2–4 as many times as necessary until the speaker has nothing more to say or as time allows.)

Validation:

1. I imagine this situation makes you feel

   _____

   (fill in the blank with your best guess about their feelings).
2. Express genuine understanding, if possible: I can see why you feel that way. (Validation is not agreement nor approval. It is merely an attempt to understand.)

Resolution:

1. What do you want or need from me?

    Possible solutions:

    - I just needed to be heard. That is enough.
    - I need a hug.
    - I need comfort.
    - I want an apology.
    - I need to problem solve with you.
    - I want your advice.
    - I don't want any advice.
    - I need space and time away from you.
    - I need to agree to disagree.
    - I want to come to a compromise with you.
    - I want you to pray for me.

2. I hear that you want_____.

    I am able to do _____.

    (There is no guarantee that the listener can fulfill the
    needs of the speaker. It is okay and necessary for the
    listener to let the speaker know what can and cannot
    be done in response to the request.)

The structure of these steps safeguards the experience of
the speaker and gives the listener the necessary guardrails to
attune to the speaker's experience. When a person is afraid,

the natural tendency is to tell them, "It's okay, don't be afraid." Although this response is meant to comfort, it actually invalidates the person's feelings and shuts them down. A more healing response would be, "Tell me about your fear."

Likewise, when one is sad, the natural response is, "Don't cry." I abhor that phrase because it interferes with the God-given, healing nature of sadness and tears. One of the biological functions of tears includes a release of biotoxins produced by emotional stress built up in the body due in part to the natural stress-response cycle. A more effective response to tears would be, "It's okay to cry. I want to hear about your sorrow." Emotions hold meaning. When we can be patient enough to draw out their meaning, they can be resolved, and we experience a resulting physical and emotional release and relief.

On many occasions, my children's disobedient behavior has been annoying. Their moodiness and obstinacy didn't make sense in the circumstances, especially if we were doing something that was nice and enjoyable for them!

In these instances, the Comfort Circle has never failed to reveal a deeper emotional struggle. For instance, once when my son was mysteriously moody, I invited him into the Comfort Circle. He disclosed that he was wrestling with a fear that his daddy would die and we would be left unprotected in our home. He imagined that bad guys would break in and attack us! When diving into my daughter's unusually gloomy attitude recently, she revealed that she fears her brothers don't love her and don't want to play with her. She was feeling lonely and worried that they would never include her again.

Sometimes it only takes about ten minutes to help my children identify underlying fears and hurts of which they weren't even fully aware and which I could never have guessed. My act of listening, being fully present, and offering comfort and solutions eases their minds and often restores their normally cheerful, cooperative, obedient spirits.

As a psychologist, I like to think I'm pretty skilled at noticing emotional difficulty and getting to the root of it. But on some days, in my own home, with the people I love the most, I can see only that my children are agitating me and that they should shape up, get over it, and get back in line. And I really just want to flip on a show or video game to shut them up. I want to unplug from my unpleasant reality by plugging my kids and myself into digital distraction. But how much richer it is to lean into the discomfort and actually resolve it! Please join me in applying the Comfort Circle to peel back the surface layer and find the emotional pain underneath, instead of relying on screens to just get through it.

On another occasion, Henry was unusually grumpy, surly, and disrespectful. When we allowed him to use the computer or watch a cartoon, he was fine. As soon as the digital distraction was off, the disrespect and disobedience continued. We ended up sending him to his room for a time out. Later, I checked on him and found him in tears. I engaged in the Comfort Circle with an invitation:

"Henry, I can see that you are upset. I'd like to hear about how you are feeling."

"I'm mad at you and Daddy because you sent me to my room and you won't let me watch any more cartoons," he said.

I reflected, "So, you're upset with us because we gave you a time out. What else?"

"I don't like when Daddy is mad at me. Sometimes I'm scared."

"Daddy's anger scares you?"

"Yeah, it makes me think that he is sick of me."

"Oh, it makes you think that Daddy is sick of you. Henry, it makes sense that you feel angry and scared. I imagine you are also feeling sad, and I see that you are crying. What do you want from me?"

"I want you to tell Daddy."

So I told Mike and asked him to join us and offer the Comfort Circle as well. Both of my men were able to acknowledge that they had upset and hurt each other. We then prayed together, and Mike asked Henry to forgive him. Henry asked for forgiveness, too. They hugged. It felt as if we were enveloped in grace. Our listening and validating his feelings did not negate that he had been disobedient and had merited discipline; we acknowledged his experience while not excusing his bad behavior. Because we attuned to him, Henry was able to jump up and get back to his normally vivacious and kind disposition. Comfort resolved his distress, and our discipline addressed his disobedience.

Henry's annoying behavior had stopped with digital distraction. But imagine the loss of deep connection and true emotional resolution if we had only distracted him and not dug deeper. But too often, the easier solution is to do exactly that. And unfortunately, digital distraction can keep us in a pleasantly numb state, allowing us to avoid addressing the distress—whether it's our own or our children's.

Comfort is a human necessity. We are designed to thrive when we have a base of safety, knowing that we are loved and accepted. A baby's first year of life is made up of needs, distress, and cries for help. When those deficits are met with consistent, warm, and responsive comfort, a baby learns to trust through developing a secure attachment with his parents or caregivers. This pattern leads to the ability to regulate one's emotions. The combination of parental responsiveness, comfort, secure attachment, and emotional self-regulation give a child a strong chance to lead a successful life. That secure foundation formed in infancy, if built upon in like manner in the ensuing years, has even been shown to protect children from becoming vulnerable to addictive behavior during adolescence.[13]

A baby's need for comfort is obvious, but that human need becomes more subtle and less recognizable with age. Despite being a doctoral-level, licensed psychologist, I too was ignorant about recognizing and resolving my emotional distress. I had not acquired the skill of asking for comfort. When was the last time you realized you had a comfort deficit and asked someone to console you?

As parents, part of our job is to protect our children from harm and raise them to be productive citizens. This protective/teaching focus can overshadow the equally important task of comforting our children (beyond infancy). We can get so busy correcting and guiding them that we miss the chances to see their hearts and to meet them where they are. Parenting involves helping our children move forward into maturity. To do that well while maintaining relationship, it is essential to slow down and turn the screens off in order to hear and see our children. We must frequently lean close to update ourselves about the state of their hearts, their interests, hopes, fears, stresses, relationships, and ever-changing preferences. If I am constantly plugged into my computer and repeatedly responding to work through my phone, I cannot be present enough to regularly attain attunement with my family. And neither can you.

Perhaps you haven't received healthy comfort and you do not know how to give it to your child. But you can learn. It is never too late to improve while there is life and breath in our bodies. No matter how well or how poorly you have comforted your children so far, you can get better. Any improvement on your part will equip your children to regulate their emotions and handle distress without having to hide behind a screen or resort to addictive behavior.

Interrelational safety and attunement through the Comfort Circle calms the sympathetic nervous system and stimulates the parasympathetic nervous system, which brings the body into rest. In moments of warmth and comfort between two people, a bonding hormone called oxytocin is released. Oxytocin counteracts the effects of cortisol and helps the body ease into rest and relaxation. Anxiety, fear, panic, depression, anger, and resentment can be resolved or managed through experiences of emotional attunement and safety. Quality comfort from another human being is the most effective way to resolve emotional distress.

What are your memories of comfort from your family? How did your parents soothe you? Did they continue to offer you solace even as you grew older? A significant challenge of growing into healthy, capable adults is becoming and remaining aware of our physical and emotional needs and learning how to manage them rather than being controlled by them. One of a parent's primary responsibilities is to decipher their young child's needs and meet them. Over time, parents teach the child to become more self-sufficient. Ideally, we would develop a balance of meeting our own needs to the best of our ability, and we would turn to God and other safe people for those needs which we cannot satisfy on our own. Emotional needs are messy, and understanding them is a skill and an art. People who can do this well have strong self-regulation.

In order to develop character, we have to face frustration time and again and be comforted and reassured that we will overcome it. Self-regulation cannot be developed in the absence of trying emotions. When children are saved from frustration too quickly and too often through digital distraction, they miss the opportunities to develop this critical skill.

The Comfort Circle is a simple and effective tool that aids us in developing emotional resolution and self-regulation. It works best when eye contact is made and distractions are kept at bay. Phones, televisions, and computers all interfere with the physical bonding process.

Your challenge is to approach your children individually. Ask them to tell you about something that is distressing them. If they are willing to talk, listen to them by using the Comfort Circle steps. If this approach is foreign for your family, expect that it may not go well at first. Your children may decline to talk with you at all. They may be turned off by this odd new approach. They may find that such a structured conversation is too awkward. It will probably feel disingenuous to you and to them at first. Accept their "no" if they will not yet participate. But don't give up. Try again in a few days.

For some families, I recommend that the conversation should be prefaced by an explanation. "I'm trying to learn how to be a better listener. I know I tend to give you too much advice and lecturing. Would you let me try listening to you in a different way today? It will be brief and we can stop at any point. It will probably feel odd, but I think it will help us both. Can we give it a shot?" For others, I recommend skipping the explanation and just getting right into it. Neither way is the only right way. Feel free to try both.

The Comfort Circle is so effective at opening up the heart that unwelcome feelings of vulnerability can surface if emotional or verbal mistreatment has occurred in the past. In those situations, it is best to practice first and troubleshoot with a therapist.

If there has been significant discord between you and your children, broken trust, or abuse, you may need a therapist to help guide you into the Comfort Circle.

We are designed to receive comfort in relationship, and if we don't find it there, we will seek to quench that lifelong thirst with anything that will ease our discomfort. These days, we are seeing that—at startlingly young ages—our children are finding comfort in digital addiction, pornography, and substance use. But we can model and teach them how to access comfort in a healthy, sustainable, life-giving way.

Because comfort from another person is not always available, it behooves our children to teach them alternative forms of non-digital coping. Reading and exercise, like relational comfort, have been scientifically shown to calm the body's nervous system, lower heart rate, and reduce stress, anxiety, and depression.[14] Reading fiction enhances brain connectivity, improves vocabulary, and increases empathy.[15] I recommend that parents try reading a few pages to their children at breakfast (when you have a captive audience). Books at bedtime are a good replacement for late-night screen use. Reading paper books in the evening prepares the body for sleep in a way that screens, with their blue light, cannot. Regular trips to the library are a budget friendly way to keep a stack of new reading material beside your children's beds for nighttime reading.

Exercise decreases cortisol and epinephrine levels, thus combating the effects of stress. Exercise also decreases symptoms of depression and anxiety and has been shown to be as effective as anti-depressant medication for mild to moderate depression.[16] I recommend inviting your children for a short walk in the evening; even once around the block is a good start.

My fervent hope is that, more than anything else, this book will help you to build a better relationship with your children. A stable, consistent parental relationship is a cornerstone upon which a child's future will be constructed. We are designed to survive, recover, and thrive in the safety and comfort of relationship. Suffering and tribulation are a guaranteed part of the human experience; comfort, tragically, is not guaranteed. But we can change that. Let's.

CHAPTER 3

Self-Control

S elf-control is the ability to override an impulse or desire by suppressing one goal in order to pursue another.[1] When it comes to screens (and life in general), self-control is a quintessential skill we parents must master so that we can impart it to our children. It involves delaying gratification and restraining impulsivity. It sacrifices current superficial pleasure for sometimes delayed profound happiness.

Parental expectation, warmth, and modeling strongly affect how quickly children develop self-control. The earlier in life that the self-control muscle is strengthened, the better the long-term results. Self-control influences the quality of one's health, education, relationships, and finances. It impacts whether one will engage in addiction or criminal behavior in adolescence and adulthood.[2] Our children remain under our supervision for such a relatively short time; the days are long, but the years are short. Are we preparing them now to make good choices, especially in our absence, by developing self-control?

If you learned about a potent, simple means to develop self-control, would you want to try it? What if it only required practicing a very doable activity for just a few minutes, four times per week? This technique was revealed to me several years ago, and I have since made it a habit for myself and my family. We are far from perfect, but we are experiencing some success worth celebrating and sharing. Read on!

Do you know your children's temptations, inclinations, and weaknesses online and offline? Do you intentionally address them together? What grade would you give yourself and each of your children in the exercise of self-control?

In my family, we are all tempted to take the easier route. We would prefer entertainment over academics and chores. Some of my children lack a cartoon satiation point. If they could watch or play video games all day every day, they might. We Bentons are inclined to procrastinate, and we want to cut corners on the difficult tasks. We like to argue and prove that we are right and you are wrong. If you catch us in our mistakes, we will want to minimize, lie, and make excuses to cover up. And those are just some of our ugly propensities.

Self-control is not an inborn, inherent skill. Babies come into the world with little to none of it. They do not have the ability to control their voices, movements, or their bodily functions. Children can develop the ability to control themselves, their emotions, and their behavior, with the potential for significant improvements, around the time they enter kindergarten and elementary school. During these years, expectations of self-regulation increase and the frontal lobe of the brain develops. But as we can easily see from our culture, these physical changes do not automatically result in more self-control.

Some rebellion should be expected as part of healthy childhood development. According to psychologist Erik Erikson, a natural impulse toward independence spikes during two main age ranges.[3] Every harried parent knows that between two and three years of age, a toddler begins to push away with a strengthening "no" and "mine!" as he or she develops autonomy. Individual identity is further defined from twelve to eighteen years old as teens test out who they are in comparison and opposition to their parents. When played out in a screen-saturated world, normal rebellion and curiosity acquire a whole new depth of access, exposure, and consequence.

If my husband and I were not intervening with our children's proclivities, how would they handle themselves? When Junie was six years old, I asked her, "If you had a day to do whatever you wanted with the iPad, what would you do?" She asked how many hours are in a day and then replied, "I would watch cartoons for twelve hours, but I would probably need to take eleven breaks for snacks and sippers and to go to the bathroom. Maybe I would get a headache if I watched cartoons all day." If your children were left unsupervised, what would they do online and offline?

A survey conducted in 2009 found that 50.2 percent of teens acknowledged having the desire to rebel and make unhealthy choices online and offline up to ten times daily.[4]

We might extrapolate that information to surmise that in a single day, our children will come to multiple crossroads of healthy and unhealthy options. Here's a potential typical day in the life of a student attending virtual school.

Time of Day	Crossroads Choice
8 a.m.–2 p.m.	To be tardy for online classes, tilt the camera away while snoozing, secretly chat with friends, and watch unrelated entertainment videos throughout the school day (unbeknownst to the teachers).
2 p.m.	To frivolously spend money on digital weapons for an online game with a one-click option linked to Mom and Dad's credit card.

Time of Day	Crossroads Choice
3 p.m.	To join a group of kids ganging up on and making fun of a peer on social media. To check the most recent posts of photos and videos of other kids cutting themselves and discussing thoughts of death and suicide.
4 p.m.	To click on that titillating advertisement of a very attractive, mostly naked underage girl.
5 p.m.	To send a sexual selfie to a guy whose acquaintance was just made on Tinder.
6 p.m.	To spend the evening binge-watching a favorite TV-MA-rated show, check the latest videos of some highly sexualized young YouTube influencers, and then play *Fortnite* and *Grand Theft Auto* until midnight in the privacy of the bedroom.
12 a.m.	To stay up for another three hours snapchatting, then leave a Facetime call with the boyfriend/girlfriend on for the remaining hours of the night so that they can virtually "sleep together."

Our children will be—and perhaps already have been—inclined, invited, and tempted to do all these things and more! I didn't pull these examples out of thin air, folks. That is what our worldly culture offers at the click of a button and in the blink of an eye. What can we parents do to instill the ability to practice self-control in kids who inhabit a world that often celebrates out-of-control behavior?

My husband and I are determined to fight these battles to uphold our values and to guide our children to do the same (as much as it lies within our limited power). I am sure that is your desire as well. All of us must choose whether to exercise the self-control muscle so we can build it up and take authority over our bodies, minds, emotions, resources, and lives. Parental modeling of self-restraint is necessary but insufficient. We parents must train our children to master self-control.

I have engaged in years of research and study to find out how best to master my baser desires in order to be successful in this war and how to translate that into parenting. I have found and applied some unexpected answers, with great results, that I want to share with you.

The secret-sauce component to self-control has been sitting in front of our noses all this time. Its supernatural ability to empower us to control our impulses is infrequently mentioned, even in faith communities. From birth to my late twenties, I attended Catholic Mass weekly, and for some periods daily, in churches across the world. I have attended Christian worship services weekly since 2012. I regularly listen to sermons and talks from pastors and Christian speakers. But I have never heard the following information preached from the pulpit. NEVER:

Research shows that interacting with the Bible (reading, listening, or discussing it) at least four times weekly increases self-restraint and protects marriages and families from all kinds of destructive behavior—including divorce, infidelity, pornography, substance abuse, violence, and unhealthy levels of anger.[5]

Do you have your own Bible? Do you know where it is? When did you last dust it off and crack it open? When did you last read it to your children? Do they read it for themselves? For most of us, the answer is "rarely, if ever." Only 35.1 percent of Americans report reading the Bible at all. Only 13.9 percent engage with Scripture at least four days per week. Those numbers aren't much better among believers. Only 28.8 percent of Christians report touching Scripture at least four days per week, according to surveys conducted by the Center for Bible Engagement (CBE).[6]

Hold on to your seats for the astounding stats about the Bible's power to influence our behavior. Those who engage with the Word at least four days per week are 57 percent less likely to drink to the point of inebriation; 68 percent less likely to engage in sex outside of marriage; and 61 percent less likely to view pornography.[7] It seems that the frequency of four days—more than half the week—is an essential tipping point. Three days or fewer of Bible reading is beneficial, but the effect on self-control is significantly less.

Studies reveal that the children of religious parents (Christian, Jewish, and Muslim) tend to demonstrate more self-control, are less impulsive, and are more conscientious and agreeable than children raised in nonreligious families.[8] Attending worship services and praying show positive effects on children's behavior, but reading Scripture has the most significant impact and is the best predictor of whether our children will choose the fun, easy way of the world or the more difficult choice of self-control and obedience to authority. Young people who report regularly reading the Bible have the lowest rates of involvement in risky behavior such as poor online decisions, drinking, smoking, stealing, destructive thoughts, violence, and premarital sex.[9]

My mom read Bible stories to me and my siblings as young children, but the practice petered out in elementary school. Unfortunately, neither my siblings nor I continued the habit as adolescents. I don't recall my parents encouraging us to read the Bible. Going to Mass regularly was a much higher priority for our Catholic family than reading Scripture. I believed that skipping Sunday Mass was a mortal sin that could result in the loss of my salvation. I thought reading Scripture was optional.

For most of my life, I saw the Bible as an important historical text documenting the development of Judaism and Christianity. It seemed sufficient that I heard it read in weekly Mass. I was ignorant about its supernatural power to transform my own thinking. Furthermore, I had only been familiar with the King James version, written in the beautiful but antiquated style, which for me was esoteric and taxing to read. I had never gotten much farther than the begats and the temple measurements. I admire any of you who are able to appreciate the Old English version. I needed something more digestible, but didn't know it existed.

Two things occurred to change the role the Bible played in my life. First, I learned how it can protect a marriage from infidelity and divorce when Dr. Dave Stoop, a Christian psychologist, was teaching at a conference I attended. He pointed out that 20–40 percent of married couples experience infidelity and about half of all couples (Christian and non-Christian) end up divorcing. But only 1 percent of couples who pray and read the Bible more than three days per week get divorced.[10] There is a history of infidelity and pornography use in my family background, and I had a significant fear that infidelity was inevitable in my own marriage.

So this potential protection for marriage was personally, deeply meaningful and eye-opening.

Then I learned that multiple translations of the Bible exist, many written in a very readable format. When I came across a New International Version, the *Life Journey Bible*, with commentary by Drs. Henry Cloud and John Townsend, the Bible came to life for me! I could finally understand a good portion of it, and I believed that reading it would protect and strengthen my self-control and my marriage. My motivation skyrocketed and reading the Bible became a daily routine.

Knowing that engaging with Scripture will impact my children's behavior and protect the choices they make with screens fires me up and motivates me to read to them daily. I feel awkward and apprehensive about introducing activities to my children that I assume they will not find agreeable. This can result in procrastination and avoidance on my part. However, I am frequently pleasantly surprised. When my attitude is upbeat and I am gentle and firm, my children are often receptive and usually end up enjoying the process more than I anticipated.

We have tried a variety of children's Bibles and have enjoyed them all. We read Steve's book *Kirby McCook and the Jesus Chronicles*, which intertwines Scripture with a humorous fictional story of adolescents learning about faith. Months after finishing the book, my nine-year-old asked if we could read it again! Kid-friendly versions make reading the Word more enjoyable and digestible for easily distracted and bored kids.

When calling my kiddos to read with me, they sometimes ask, "Do we have to?" I simply respond "Yup," and that has been sufficient. This has been our established norm for the majority of their lives, so they don't know anything different. I'll admit, though, that occasionally, reading a Bible story is the last thing I want to do. But knowing the layer of protection it gives my family in a screen-saturated world, I am driven to be consistent.

Of course, it isn't just the act of reading that produces the fruit of self-control, but rather learning about the expectations of our Creator and digesting the supernatural content, which we'll discuss in more detail in the next chapter.

God designed us and gave us a manual that teaches us how best to live. He asks us to build the strength and ability to consistently choose what is right. He warns us that, since the Fall of Man, we have been broken and weak in character. In speaking to Adam and Eve's son Cain about his struggle with temptation, God said, "If you do not do what is right, sin is crouching at your door; it desires to have you, but you must rule over it" (Genesis 4:7). We have an inherent inclination to rebel against rules and authority and to indulge in any given pleasure or desire. Our society has become increasingly hedonistic: do what pleases you, when it pleases you, just because it pleases you.

God has always been in the business of eudaemonism: happiness as a byproduct of the pursuit of long-term goals and character growth. Put another way, if we do the right thing first, we experience abundance and blessings because of obedience and self-control. Through the Bible, God speaks directly about the process of developing self-restraint. It is accessible to us through His Spirit, which "does not make us timid, but gives us power, love, and self-discipline" (2 Timothy 1:7). It is one of several fruits produced by the Holy Spirit, including "love, joy, peace, forbearance, kindness, goodness, faithfulness, gentleness, and self-control" (Galatians 5:22–23). As we seek Him through His Word, He will give us (and our children) "the desire and power to do what pleases Him" (Philippians 2:13 NLT). When we do not know what to do, if we ask God for wisdom, He will give it to us generously (James 1:5). In fact, He promises to "meet all [our] needs according to the riches of His glory in Christ Jesus" (Philippians 4:19). The Word of God is "alive and active" (Hebrews 4:12). We can request and receive His power in our lives and for our children through the action of engaging with Him through His book.

Did you already know about those promises? Do your children know them? Despite being a believer all my life, I was ignorant until I started reading the Bible and sharing it with my children. Pastor Rick Warren of Southern California's Saddleback Church explains that God's promises are like a check written out to us, just waiting for us to cash it in and receive His blessings. But in our ignorance, most of us never even discover the check exists.

Guiding our children to engage with Scripture at least four times per week is a very tall order, but it offers the best chance of building their self-control muscle so that they will use digital media responsibly. Even if you are part of the 64.9 percent of Americans who don't read the Bible regularly, aren't you feeling a little inspired and motivated right now to initiate regular Scripture time with your family? If Bible time has not been a habitual family practice, it can be overwhelming to consider coaxing your children to pick up the unlikely behavior of reading the Word. Allow me to suggest several approaches that have worked for my family.

Steps to Build Bible Time

Pray for God's help and admit that you have not been reading His book enough yourself, let alone guiding your children to do so. You might say, "Lord, You know I want to raise my kids well. Sometimes I don't know what to do to get them to behave right, especially when it comes to their screens. And I feel like I'm running out of time and energy to do much differently at this point. If it is true that reading the Bible might help my kids, I'll need Your help. They won't want to read it. I don't even really want to read it. But I do want to teach them self-control. Please give me the desire to follow through on this."

Start reading it on your own first. Let your children notice your change, which will hopefully inspire and pique their interest.

We enjoy family viewing of *The Chosen*, a show about the life of Christ. It expands on the gospels with realistic fictional additions that enhance rather than detract from the Bible stories of the life of Christ. It is a visual and auditory engagement with Scripture. (The episodes are free to view and can be found at https://watch.angelstudios.com/thechosen.) Warning: the first few episodes of the first season depict Mary Magdalene's struggle with demonic possession, so we skipped to the third episode because our children are young.

In a process that paralleled writing this book, I felt nudged to select just a verse or story summary from my solo Bible time to later share with my children. I write the verse down along with a few questions to promote family discussion. The devotion ends with a personalized prayer for my kids. The note is only a few sentences long. I leave it out on the table for my husband, who reads it with the kids at breakfast. It could be completed in under three minutes, but the kids' participation often stretches it out to five or ten minutes, by their choice! They always have something to share in answer to the questions. We find mealtimes to be ideal for family devotions given that we have a hungry, captive audience. I have combined these brief discussion guides into a booklet, *100 Days of Biblical Family Engagement*. It can be found at www.dralicebenton.com.

God's nudge for me to pen the devotions included asking my husband to lead rather than doing it all myself. This aspect is important and merits further explanation. Our Creator designed families to ideally have a principal leader (the father) and a secondary leader (the mother). We parents are to be coleaders, but wives are asked to allow our husbands to be the primary leaders, especially in matters of spirituality. This is obviously quite countercultural and does not come naturally to most of us.

My family was spiritually matriarchal, and my husband's family did not engage in many parent-guided spiritual practices. I am more aware of and driven to guide our family's spirituality, and I have more experience and training. My husband would be happy to let me lead. It had not occurred to him to do so on his own, and he has not had the training to be our spiritual leader. I tend to be more vigilant and conscientious about our children's faith growth. It would be much simpler for me to retain leadership. It goes smoothly when I am in charge of our spiritual practices. But the last thing the enemy wants is for God's order to reign in our home. Satan would much prefer I take the path of least resistance. My spiritual obligation is to build my husband up as our leader, and to restrain myself. Our family will benefit more in the long run as my husband and I work to submit to God's design of leadership. So I try to stay in the role of the spiritual production manager. I work behind the scenes to make sure things happen, but I ask my husband to have the on-scene presence and leadership.

My husband does not agree with my opinion about the importance of him being the spiritual leader. He wonders if I am trying to apply antiquated cultural norms from an outdated patriarchal society, as presented in the Old Testament. He is not convinced that God needs or wants him to lead our spiritual charge, especially when it comes so naturally to me. If I'm better at it and want to initiate it, why not let me?

Given our difference in opinion, I am that much more grateful that he participates in the morning devotional time.

Our simple devotional time has redeemed the start of our day and protects the time from the kids' bickering and arguing. Previously, our children sat to eat breakfast on their own while my husband and I prepared for the day. Nitpicking and arguments frequently broke out. These days, passersby are now likely to hear a bit of solid discussion about God drifting from our dining room rather than squabbling. I credit the change to the fact that we are inviting Him to the table each day. To my surprise, our kids are curious and responsive to devotions and even request them when we miss a day!

Recently, Henry saw me preparing a passage for devotions and said, "Mom, would you please let me do one?" He selected a verse, asked me for some ideas, and then led us that morning at breakfast! I am witnessing unexpected breakthrough, powered by God's Word.

Let's consider another option for developing time for Scripture. While my husband leads off the morning devotional, I close the day by reading a brief Bible story to the kids as part of our bedtime routine. When Henry was young, we started off with children's Bibles. *Five-Minute Nighttime Bible Stories* has great illustrations, and the limited amount of time was doable for me at the end of a long day. We have graduated to the *Action Bible*, a comic book–style format that is interesting and attractive to Henry as a nine-year-old. As we finish one version, I look for other styles that will hopefully hold the kids' attention and give them a different angle on God's Word. I bring Bible story books home from the library from time to time to add variety and maintain interest.

Buy a translation that is appealing, eye-catching, and age-appropriate for your children. Pray for the right words that will best reach their hearts as you introduce this new routine to them.

You might broach the topic with, "Hey, I love you and want to spend time with you. I'm learning that reading the Bible will help us to make healthy choices in our lives and have better self-control. I know I need that. We both know I get irritated easily and then I can be snippy with you. I want to be better for you and our family. I need to apologize to you that I haven't done this with you enough before. Would you forgive me?

"Is there anything about yourself that you'd like to control better? Would you be willing to read it with me once this week for a few minutes? Which day and time would work best for you?"

Perhaps your child responds by saying, "What? Are you crazy? I don't want to. This is super weird. Why do we have to do this all of a sudden? My friends' parents don't make them do this." Validation and acknowledgement go a long way in these cases. "You are right. This is weird, and it is sudden. Most people don't do this. I don't blame you for not wanting to do it at all. I understand that you would rather not. But we both know that you are already facing a lot of tough choices with what is available to you online and offline. I'm learning that reading this old book together is what will best help us make healthy choices. So I've decided we need to start checking it out. You can decide when and how much time we spend reading it."

"Mom, I refuse to read this with you. I just won't do it." When I hear things like this, one of my favorite parenting aces in the hole is to link my request to the leverage I hold as their parent. I tend to apply this strategy as a last resort in the face of obstinate resistance from my children. It is helpful to acknowledge that I really can't force them to do much of anything, but I can limit their access to my resources to enhance their willingness. "Okay. I can't make you do it and I won't force you to. I want you to know that you are welcome to continue to enjoy

_____" (fill in the blank with whichever one of the following options is important to your child: the phone, computer, the gaming equipment, money, car, etc.) "once you cooperate with me. I'll check back with you in a few days."

Then stick to your decision. Making an empty threat is useless and detrimental. If you don't follow through, your children learn they can ignore you. Brace yourself to be labeled the "mean, boring parent." But your children's anger is well worth the protection these steps will provide for them and their use of screens.

Make the experience as pleasant as possible while bracing yourself for your children's displeasure. For the first encounter, you might provide their favorite fancy drink and pastry. Express gratitude. Be curious. Allow whatever emotions your children might experience, especially dislike of the activity. "Thank you for sitting down with me. I know you didn't want to do this, but you showed up anyhow. What did you think of it? What did you like and dislike?" Do not allow a negative reaction to dictate your action. Validate their experience while holding to your conviction:

"Mom, this is so boring. Do we really have to do this again?"

"I can understand that this is boring for you, and you'd rather not do it again. I believe this will strengthen us, protect us, and bless us. So, yes, it is important enough to do it again."

I am inclined to give my children as much decision-making power as possible. This will prepare them better for taking authority over their own lives. We cannot and should not try to force our children to choose our beliefs or practices, but we should do our best to influence them to choose the right path. We cannot make them enjoy the process. So let's do our best to influence and leverage (if need be) rather than demand. We can trust that as we obey Him, God will do the work within us and our children to ignite interest and desire, and to cultivate self-control in us and in our kids. Even God will allow our children to accept or reject Him and His way. As we model and guide rather than force, the better the chance that our children will choose Him of their own accord.

Start small. Hope for the best and brace for the worst. I pray for God's success to shine through your willingness.

CHAPTER 4

Reset Your Expectations

How would you describe your parenting style? Are you emotionally warm or somewhat aloof? Do you prefer to be the decision maker or to take a more communal approach? Do you and your spouse complement or clash in your philosophies? How have you determined the rules for your family? How do you communicate them to your children?

Scientists have studied and identified four main parenting styles. They have differentiated the most effective approaches with the best long-range outcomes for children, as well as the more ineffective and even destructive approaches.[1] You might be surprised by the findings.

Parenting Style	Characteristics	Outcome for Children
Authoritative	• High Expectation • Warm Emotional Engagement	• Secure Attachment • Strong Self-Regulation • High Performance • Low Susceptibility to Addictive Behavior
Permissive	• Low Expectation • Warm Emotional Engagement	• Secure Attachment • Moderate Self-Regulation • Moderate Susceptibility to Addictive Behavior
Authoritarian	• High Expectation • Little Emotional Engagement • Harsh, Demanding	• Insecure Attachment • Low Self-Regulation • High Susceptibility to Addictive Behavior • High Susceptibility to Rebellious Behavior
Neglectful	• Low Expectation • Little Emotional Engagement	• Impaired Self-Regulation • Low Performance • High Susceptibility to Addictive Behavior • High Susceptibility to Violent Behavior

Authoritative parenting builds the most stable base for healthy future behavior and offers the best likelihood of success for children. This approach combines strong expectations with sensitivity and consideration for children's feelings and opinions, and appears to be facilitated by participation in a belief system and practices. Authoritative parents are demanding but flexible.[2] Children in these homes tend to have a secure attachment to their parents. The long-range results usually include higher academic performance, good self-control, low susceptibility to addictive behavior and substance use, strong relationships, good financial management, and even better physical health.[3] Authoritative parenting and the Mentor approach to screens are crossover styles with similarities in parent-led structure with flexibility for children's opinions.

Permissive parents are strong in emotional warmth and weak in expectations. They are likely to raise children with an emotionally secure attachment style, but with higher susceptibility to substance use, addictive behaviors, ingratitude, and entitlement than children of authoritative parents.[4]

Authoritarian parents take a dictator-like approach, demanding compliance and enforcing strict discipline. Neglectful parents are hands-off and emotionally absent. Children of authoritarian and neglectful parents tend to have the worst outcomes, including insecure attachment, poor self-regulation, and high likelihood of addictive behavior, substance use, rebellion, and violence.

Many parents are a blend of more than one style.

The techniques we've discussed up to this point will help develop and strengthen warmth and responsiveness. Now, we'll take a closer look at how to develop, discuss, and enforce high expectations for our children.

Religious parents (including Christian, Jewish, and Muslim) appear to be uniquely equipped to take an authoritative approach.⁵ We know that engagement with Scripture protects children, families, and marriages from unhealthy behavior. So now, let's unpack what the Bible says about God's expectations for us, what we should ask of our children, and whether it is relevant for our digital behavior.

The most basic rules outlined in Scripture are the Ten Commandments. So pop quiz, hotshot, how many of the commandments can you recall right now? Come on, count 'em off on your fingers. Do your children know them? I was able to recall nine on the spot, and my children knew five commandments. These are arguably God's clearest guidelines for humanity. And my family and I don't even have them all memorized!

How often do you talk about God and His standards in your home? Do your children know that you expect your household to uphold His ways? In the process of writing this book, I have been newly motivated to address God's standards more frequently with my children. I'm certain we can all improve in this area.

God details where and how often His way should be discussed with our children: at home, on the road, going to bed, and getting up (Deuteronomy 6:7). The Israelites were exhorted to learn the Law and teach it to their children so that they would listen, learn to fear God, and follow it (Deuteronomy 31:12). In the Old Testament, Moses's successor, Joshua, was told that if he would meditate on the Law day and night, keeping it always on his lips so that he could obey it, he would be prosperous and successful (Joshua 1:7–9). And who doesn't want that for their family?

In case you haven't reviewed them in a while, the commandments are found in the book of Exodus (20:1–17). They are numbered and presented in different ways by different religions and denominations. I will present them in the Jewish format. They are as follows:

1. I am the Lord Your God, who brought you out of Egypt, out of the land of slavery. You shall have no other gods before Me. You shall not make for yourself an image. You shall not bow down to them or worship them.

2. You shall not misuse the name of the Lord your God.

3. Remember the Sabbath by keeping it holy. Six days you shall labor and do all your work, but the seventh day is a Sabbath to the Lord, your God. On it you shall not do any work.

4. Honor your father and mother so that you may live long in the land the Lord your God is giving you.

5. You shall not murder.

6. You shall not commit adultery.

7. You shall not steal.

8. You shall not give false testimony against your neighbor.

9. You shall not covet your neighbor's house.

10. You shall not covet your neighbor's wife or anything that belongs to your neighbor.

Do these rules seem antiquated and irrelevant? They probably do to your older children. They apply today as much as ever, and particularly with our children's online activity. They perfectly encapsulate the necessary modern guardrails to guide our children's activity online and offline. Let's analyze their relevance.

1. I am the Lord Your God, who brought you out of Egypt, out of the land of slavery. You shall have no other gods before me. You shall not make for yourself an image. You shall not bow down to them or worship them.

First and foremost, we are reminded that God is our rescuer. Then we are told not to set anything above God in importance or worship. God is to have prominence in our lives. What He says goes. This necessarily precedes the rest of the commandments because a recognition of God as good, desiring our freedom, and as the highest authority undergirds the importance of the rest of the commandments. This answers the eternal questions, "Why do I have to? Says who?"

Acknowledging that God is God means keeping Him as our top priority, believing He has our best interests in mind, and thus being willing to obey what He asks of us. If we respect His authority and justice system, we are more likely to obey Him.

Consider how misbehaving children, when watching something inappropriate, close the video when an adult enters the room. Bad behavior stops because of the perpetrator's fear of an authority figure. That fear is a knowledge and respect for the fact that consequences may be meted out. It is a healthy motivator that all humans need in our broken state. What better than to teach our children that THE AUTHORITY cares about them, and always sees their actions online and offline, especially in parental absence? That healthy fear must be instilled; humans are not born with it. It must be taught for the sake of behavior modification. And our children need to know the long-term consequences of their behavior in their relationship with God. Experimental studies have confirmed that when we think we are being watched by a Deity, our behavior improves.[6]

Fear is an immature motivator that will ideally develop into obedience motivated by love. We grow into obeying because we know God loves us and we trust that His mandates are in our best interests. Jesus explains that we are to love God with all of our heart, mind, soul, and strength (Mark 12:30). As we mature, perfect love drives out fear (1 John 4:18). God promises an abundance of His love if we will obey Him (Exodus 20:6) while warning that despite our obedience, sometimes even because of our obedience, we will also experience trials and tribulations (John 16:33; Matthew 10:22).

If we want our children to obey us, we must teach them that God is the Ultimate Authority over all, parents included. We should frequently redirect our children to Him. When they complain about our digital rules and expectations, we can validate that it is frustrating. Nonetheless, we have decided that, "as for me and my household, we will serve the LORD" (Joshua 24:15). Our children do not ultimately answer to parents but rather to our Heavenly Father.

When our children are disobedient in their digital activity, my husband and I strive to stand in the gap, enforce God's principles, and point our children back to Him. "Junie, I gave you permission to watch three cartoons, after which you were supposed to check in with me. I noticed that you watched five cartoons. That is too bad that you chose to disobey. When you disobey me, do you know who else you are disobeying? That's right, it's God. So, let's pray together, we need His help. 'God, we are both disobedient to You at times. Please help us to obey You and help my children to obey me. In Jesus's name. Amen.' It's too bad that you will miss dessert tonight, Junie, as a consequence."

1. We calmly acknowledge the bad behavior.
2. We pray aloud with our children for them and for ourselves in the struggle.
3. We remind them of God's standard and ask Him to help all of us to meet it better the next time, by His grace.
4. We enforce a consequence.

We want our children to learn the lesson of obeying God and obeying authority in small matters (cartoons) so that they have a better chance of doing it in more significant behavior later in life (e.g., whether to access pornography). The magnitude of misbehavior and the consequences increase with age. So, the earlier we set the stage for them to know that God and parents are in charge, the better for all involved. Even if our children don't choose to accept God's position of authority, it is still our parental duty to inform them.

Now, let's unpack idol worship. How does it apply in our modern world? Worshipping an idol is not limited to bowing down to a statue. Rather, it encompasses the things in our life to which we give the most importance, time, attention, and responsiveness.

Think of a good servant and his obedience to his master. Day or night, the master can ring for the servant and expect an immediate response. In your life, who can interrupt anything you are doing with the ring of a bell? Who pulls your strings? To whom or what are you so attached that you take him, her, or it everywhere (even into the bathroom)?

Smartphone, anyone? Are you a slave to your phone and the alerts it gives you? Does it hold a hypnotic power over you? Do you obediently check it multiple times a day without blinking an eye?

You might think this an exaggeration, but we have to ask ourselves: *Do my kids and I interact with our phones more than we interact with God? Do we check in with our phones more than we check in with God? Do we give more of our time, attention, energy, and money to our phones than we do to God?*

We all have an embarrassing number of "yes" answers there. People say they cannot go a day without their phones. Who says, "I can't go a day without God"?

If we neglect to establish God as the authority and the ultimate recipient of our worship and obedience, something else will fill that void. Woe to the child who is his own authority with license to engage in anything he might desire on his smartphone! I'll take it a scary step farther: There is only one throne in our hearts. We get to decide who will reign in our lives. There are only two choices: God and not God. If we fill that throne with anything that is not God, by default Satan gets the throne.[7]

2. You shall not misuse the name of the Lord your God.

There are several layers to this commandment. The first is the literal application of using the name of God disrespectfully and in cursing. In our culture, "Oh my God" is an acceptable proclamation of surprise to mundane matters. "Jesus Christ" can be thrown out as an expression of anger, sometimes with the F-word in the middle. While these examples may not seem important, they are subtle ways of stripping respect from the names of the Almighty. The language young people use while texting with each other is often loaded with these phrases and many other expletives. Left unchecked, this verbal disrespect will likely deteriorate into other behavior that also disrespects God. Let us impress upon our children how much their words matter, both spoken and written in the online environment from which they will never be erased.

It was difficult for me to challenge my son when I noticed him beginning to say, "Oh my God" with his peers. I hesitated to address it, feeling like a super-sensitive, over-the-top mother and worrying what other adults would think of me. But my belief in the righteousness of the utmost respect for God helped me to push through my people-pleasing, conflict-avoiding tendencies. Privately, I pointed it out to Henry and asked him to become more aware and stop saying it. I informed him that I would help him with consequences if necessary.

For approximately two weeks the following scene took place frequently. "Oh my God!" "Oops, Henry, you said it again. That's too bad. Take a break on the stairs." He would sit for several minutes and eventually apologize. "Henry, let's pray, 'God, help us to respect Your name.' Okay, would you like to try again?" The discipline succeeded and the behavior is no longer a problem.

The second layer to this commandment is calling one-self a follower of Christ, but then unrepentantly engaging in immoral behavior. When Christians misbehave online and offline, it affects the name of God. Christian youth who are willing to protect a classmate being bullied online, who choose not to curse on social media, and who choose not to use pornography, bring honor to the name of God.

Discuss with your children: What do we do online and offline that brings honor to God's name? What have we done that dishonors God's name?

3. Remember the Sabbath day by keeping it holy. Six days you shall labor and do all your work, but the seventh day is a Sabbath to the Lord, your God. On it you shall not do any work.

God commands us to rest from work and set a day apart to honor Him. Honoring Him includes gathering in community to worship and to be reminded of His ways. We were designed to work best in community—in intimate relationship with trustworthy companions all striving to live by the same godly standards.

Parents have asked me if they should allow their dissatisfied teen to reject church altogether. Is it really a battle worth fighting? My answer is an emphatic yes, it is worth taking a strong stand on this issue! With every additional year, a teen becomes 13 percent more likely to engage in risky behavior such as premarital sexual activity, substance use, and pornography. But church attendance decreases the odds of making those choices by 62 percent![8]

Expecting (and insisting, if necessary) that children participate in a church program geared specifically to them increases the likelihood of healthy peers and other adults adding a protective layer to their screen-saturated world. They are likely to hear the same messages about healthy screen use their parents have been giving them repeated and supported by others. Doesn't it drive you crazy when your children buy in to your message only when it comes from an outside source?

If your child rebels against going to church, consider allowing as much power in choosing as possible while maintaining your requirement for participation. You might say, "I've been thinking about how you dislike going to church. I bet you are exhausted after your tough school week and just want to sleep in. I know you have friends who don't have to attend. I also realize you don't care for the service I've been choosing. So, I want to strategize with you and let you make some choices for yourself. I'm willing to look at different days, times, a youth service rather than an adult service, even different churches, if need be, within reason. I do need you to participate in a Christian service, but I want to give you a lot of power over the details. I'd also like to take you out for a meal after the service, and I want you to choose where we go."

Share the decision-making power with your children within the parameters of your standards. This should be done more and more as they approach the age of eighteen, to the point that they should be making most of the decisions for their lives as long as they are choosing responsibly and respectfully.

The Sabbath rest or the Lord's Day has traditionally been a day of connecting to family and friends. Keeping the Sabbath gives an opportunity to propose a family activity that does not include screens. Our brains need a break from school, work, and digital media. You might invite your children this way: "I want us to spend an hour or two together as a family this coming Sunday. I need your help in planning it. Let's come up with a few screen-free activities that you are interested in doing. We'll take your ideas and decide together what we can do this time." Expect resistance. Roll with it by validating their annoyance and gently persisting on arranging family time.

A vital and often-overlooked part of this commandment is what God tells us to do the other six days of the week: Work![9] "Six days you shall labor and do all your work, but the seventh day is a Sabbath day" (Exodus 20:9–10). Workaholics must be reminded of the rest mandate. Lazy children must be reminded of the expectation that we all will be working the other six days. Remember, hard work and high expectations are good for our children.

4. Honor your father and mother so that you may live long in the land the Lord your God is giving you.

Children are told to honor (Exodus 20:12) and obey their parents (Ephesians 6:1). Those who do are promised a long, full life. We could all stand to address this more explicitly with our children. They need to know that God tells them to obey us and that our authority comes from Him.

My discussion with my children about this commandment went like this: "Did you know that God asks you to honor and obey Daddy and me? What do you think 'honor and 'obey' mean? Isn't it hard sometimes to do what we tell you? I know it is hard when we ask to you to end your screen time and do a chore. It can be annoying. I had a hard time obeying my parents, too. I would get very irritated with my mom especially. What things are the hardest for you to obey?" Then I just listened to them. I led them in praying for God's help and confessing that we don't follow this commandment perfectly.

I purposefully set up opportunities for my children to choose obedience (or disobedience) when it comes to our screen rules. In fact, it is important for them to be allowed to choose to disobey me. Yup, you read that correctly. They will make bad choices in their lives. I would rather those mistakes happen as early as possible while I can enforce consequences. The magnitude of the mistakes and the resulting cost are less severe now than they will be when they are older.

My children's disobedience used to frighten me. I thought it was my job to prevent them from disobeying. What an impossible, crazy-making setup! We cannot control our children's choices. But we can control our response to their choices. It is beneficial to allow our children the room to disobey so that we can help them grow from their failures. When they obey, our ability to trust them increases. The more we can trust them, the more freedom we should give them online and offline. When they fail, their access to the luxury resources they want should be restricted. In my view, almost all digital access is a luxury for our children that can and should be restricted or allowed depending on their obedience.

God asks obedience of us. But He doesn't force it. He allows us to choose. Then He allows us the rewards or consequences merited by our behavior. This system gives the best chance of influencing our children to choose good behavior.

5. You shall not murder.

It is easy to skim past this commandment, which only applies in extreme situations and has nothing to do with our children and their screens. Or does it? I see important application in several areas: the fatal power of words, the prevalence of social media-influenced self-harm and suicidal behavior, and TelAbortion—also known as at-home abortion, medication abortion, or self-induced abortion.

Jesus indicates that verbal mistreatment in anger may be equated with murder (Matthew 5:22). Have you ever been verbally attacked? If so, you know that words can cut deeply. Online culture has a vicious reputation for bullying, rumors, and gossip that slay the hearts of its victims and can ruin reputations. Digital media weaponizes these behaviors in a way that past generations never experienced. Rather than a rumor spreading through a class over a few days, disastrous vitriol can be spread over a school, neighborhood, and beyond in seconds. Cyberbullying can be a lethal threat. Victims and perpetrators are both more susceptible to the aftermath of increased depression, self-harm, suicidal thoughts, and suicidal behaviors.[10]

Suicidal thoughts and attempts are more frequent, severe, and widespread now than at any point in recorded history. A deadly subculture exists in social media that glorifies and teaches self-harm and suicide techniques. We should gently and boldly check in with our older children about their experience with and exposure to this danger.

We might say, "Everyone has bad days, and some people have very dark days and weeks that can lead to heavy thoughts and urges. What do you know about suicide and self-harm? What do you think is positive about suicide or self-harm? Do you know anyone who has had thoughts of self-harm or of wanting to die? Have you ever had those thoughts? Please come to me or Dad when you feel bad. It is our job to help you and keep you safe." If they admit to self-harm or suicidal thoughts, take it seriously and get in touch with a therapist as soon as possible.

Now, onto the controversial topic of abortion, particularly regarding our children's online access to TelAbortion. In some cases, the only requirements for a TelAbortion are an unwanted pregnancy, a gestational age of less than ten weeks, internet access, and a mailing address.[11] Eligible girls are invited to schedule a videoconference with a medical provider who can then confidentially mail abortion-inducing medication to the home, where the fetus can be privately exterminated and expelled. A leading research organization, Gynuity, has been working since 2003 to increase access to reproductive services to women and *girls*. Social media sites carried ads for TelAbortion and Gynuity with attractive graphics assuring minors that parental consent may not be required, so call for more information to get started.[12] In December of 2021, the FDA expanded access to abortion-inducing medication for the duration of the pandemic.[13]

We urgently need to teach our children our stance on abortion at increasingly younger ages, as it is becoming more accessible to them—even advertised to them—without our knowledge or consent. Taking an open-discussion approach, especially with older children, will help them to stay engaged rather than defensive.

"What do you know about abortion? It is very acceptable today in our culture. What do you think might be good about abortion and what might be harmful? Do you think it can help a girl in extreme circumstances like rape? Should it always be allowed, sometimes allowed, or never allowed? Should the father of the baby have a say about whether an abortion takes place?

"Do you know what God says about unborn babies in the Bible? Unborn babies are mentioned multiple times. Here are just a few examples. The Bible tells us that babies are known before they are formed in their mothers' wombs and that God already knows the purpose for their lives (Jeremiah 1:5). The book of Psalms talks about a baby being knitted together by God in the womb and being fearfully and wonderfully made (Psalm 139:13–16). Proverbs says that God hates hands that shed innocent blood (Proverbs 6:16–17). So, what do you think God would tell us about abortion today?"

My children know I believe abortion is the murder of an unborn child (in any situation) and goes against God's law. If you agree, you might tell them, "Taking the life of an unborn baby is murder. I hope you will never choose to have an abortion or support or pressure a girl to have an abortion. I hope you will not have to the face that decision. The best way to avoid it is to wait until marriage to have sex. If you ever become pregnant, or son, if you impregnate a girl and do not want to have the baby, please tell me first and allow me to help you. We all make mistakes. I will help you and love you through any mistakes."

Now do you think this commandment is relevant for your children?

6. You shall not commit adultery.

God directly warns us to avoid extramarital sexual activity. Jesus calls us to guard our eyes against lusting, which is a form of adultery in the heart (Matthew 5:28). This is a topic that most of us feel ill-prepared to address with our children, and perhaps hypocritical because we have made our own sexual mistakes. I have.

Our children are increasingly likely to experience sexual content online by the age of seven, whether they are accidentally exposed to pornography or engage in sexting. When I was a kid, I was interested in swing dancing. I was fourteen years old when I Googled "swing," hoping to improve my moves for the next school dance. I was shocked to find the top search results were about couples engaging in spouse swapping!

My daughter loves anything pink. When her brother received a sword as a gift, she wanted to purchase one for herself. She was sitting beside me as she looked up "pink sword" on Google. In my ignorance and naiveté, I did not foresee the barrage of sexual images that would be coming in the top results. She was five years old.

The British Board of Film Classification conducted a survey of 2,344 parents and youth in 2019.[14] Three-quarters of the parents reported that they did not believe their children had been exposed to pornography, but when asked, over half of the children— some as young as seven—reported that they had seen porn. Over half of the parents indicated that they had spoken with their children about porn, but most of the children could not recall the conversation. Many children who had seen sexual images disclosed viewing content that included violence, bondage, and rape.

A meta-analysis of studies published in 2018, indicated that one in seven children between eleven and seventeen years old has sent a sexually explicit text (sext). One in four has received sexts. One in eight has forwarded sexual content. One percent of children ten to eleven years old have appeared in, created, and/or received sexts.[15] Sexting has only been increasing as more children have been getting their own smartphones.

Most of our own parents probably struggled to address the topic of sex with us as children; perhaps some of them never spoke about it all! Few people have had good modeling in this area. But we can become better equipped, and an imperfect attempt is far better than no attempt at all.

We might tell our children, "I realize that I have been avoiding talking with you about sex because I feel awkward about it, and I know you probably do, too. My parents didn't talk with me about it. I want to fix my mistake with you. How would you feel about discussing this with me? Are you willing to talk now, or would you rather talk tomorrow? Do you prefer that I talk with you alone, or do you want Dad with us too? Would you tell me what you already know about sex? Do you know what God tells us about it? When do you think it is okay to have sex and how far you can or should go with kissing and touching before you have sex?

"What do you think about sexual activity online? What do you think about kids sexting or sending naked photos of themselves or others? Have you ever or would you ever sext? Do you know that sexting images of kids under eighteen is called child pornography? It is a federal crime if a person eighteen years old or older is involved in requesting, receiving, or resending the image. It can result in years of prison time. Younger teens who ask for sexual photos (even if they are asking for it from their boyfriends or girlfriends) can also face legal problems.[16]

"Sexual activity online or offline forms a physical, emotional, and spiritual attachment that is too big to handle well outside of marriage. With sexual intercourse, there is a risk of contracting a sexually transmitted disease and/or becoming pregnant before you are ready to have a baby. When a sexual dating relationship ends, there is a painful tearing apart because of the sexual bond that was formed through intercourse. Waiting for marriage is the best safeguard against all of these risks.

"God also cautions us to avoid entertaining fantasies about sex in our minds and hearts. That's a tough standard, almost impossible to maintain in our digital world. I know that sexual talk, images, movies, and clips are all over the place today. You are bombarded with it. It can be really titillating and thrilling, especially when it is online and secretive. You know I've made many mistakes—including in this area. You have probably already seen pornography, or you will soon. Would you please tell me about what you have seen? Will you share with me what you are thinking and feeling about all of this?

"Let's pray. 'God, I have made sexual mistakes. I ask for Your forgiveness. Please help me to teach my child to do better than I did. I pray for protection over their sexuality and their dating and marriage. Please protect them online and make them sensitive and motivated to turn away from sexual content. Help them to save sex for marriage.'"

It can be helpful, when age appropriate, to share some information about our own exposure. I first saw porn when I was about twelve years old, innocently flipping through the channels in a hotel room while we were on vacation. I was disgusted and intrigued by what I briefly saw. Later, I purposefully asked for permission to run ahead to the hotel room by myself (in order to sneak another peek). I might have watched for five or ten minutes before my family caught up with me. Those images were burned in my brain, and I can still see them today. I believe it to be important and beneficial to share some of our sexual mistakes (headlines, not details) with our children as age appropriate.

Our children probably will be uncomfortable, grossed out, and unwilling to talk about sex. We cannot control their response to us, and it is not our job to do so. But it is our responsibility to address the issue the best we can.

The privacy of personal screen use can lure our children into sexual speech, photos, and videos that they wouldn't pursue in the light of day offline. As parents, you well know that you can be in the same room as your child, even sitting next to them, and be unaware of their onscreen activity.

Inform your children, "It is my job to protect you from people who want to engage you sexually online and from your own curiosity to seek out sexual material. Premarital sexual activity is fun and exciting, but it is not healthy for us online or offline. In our household, we will not be looking at or sharing sexually explicit material online or offline. You are welcome to use our screens knowing that Dad and I will have access to all of your accounts. Your browsing history must be saved for us to see at any time. None of us is 100 percent trustworthy. This arrangement will help you to stay safe and to grow into being able to monitor yourself and to make good choices on your own. If you decide to make poor choices, Dad and I will take action. Please repeat this arrangement to me so that we both know you understand. Do you have any questions? Does any of this upset you?"

For younger children, I recommend a vague approach. You might say, "God wants us to take good care of our bodies. We must keep our genitals and girls' chests private. We should not look at naked photos online, and we should not show anyone outside of our family our private parts. We may not touch each others' private parts. Mom, Dad, and doctors might have to touch your private parts once in a while, but only to take care of you. We are not allowed to wrestle or tickle when we are naked."

I check in from time to time with our nine-year-old son, asking if any of his peers or teachers are talking about sex. Up to this point, I have only explained that it is God's way for moms and dads to love each other and have babies. He has not yet asked for more details. I have read children's books explaining anatomy in simple terms to all my children. I have also shared material with them that lightly explains and warns about inappropriate sexual touch. We want to maintain their innocence as long as possible while still providing enough information to keep them alert and protected.

7. You shall not steal.

Online theft is easily minimized, justified, and hidden. Subtler forms of stealing include copyright infringement and plagiarism. We need to teach our children that "copy and pasting" without citing the original author or without purchasing the rights to use images is theft. Using another author's words and representing them as one's original work is stealing and lying. The legal and academic consequences can be hefty, including fines, school suspension, and even expulsion.

Purchasing things online with parents' money without permission is also stealing. Many games feature pay-to-play upgrades and in-app purchases with just one click. These microtransactions may be hardly noticeable but over months can add up to thousands of dollars. Many of us parents have saved our credit card information in secure applications like Google Play and Kindle. It is easy for children to spend our money (ignorantly or intentionally) while remaining under the radar. Younger children or those with disabilities may not understand the concept of spending real money online. Numerous articles document parental woes when they finally realize what's been happening and tally up the total expenditures.[17] Children as young as six have charged upwards of $20,000 on virtual upgrades in gaming before parents realized what was taking place.[18]

We must teach our children about digital money, how easy it is to make purchases through their devices, and warn them of the consequences that will be enacted if they spend money without permission.

We might say, "If you want to buy anything online, talk it over first with me or Dad. We are willing to pay for what you need. We are willing to consider allowing you to buy unnecessary or luxury items with your own money with our knowledge and permission, but do not spend our money without our permission. That's stealing. If you steal from us, you will be required to pay us back with interest. Would you please repeat what I told you so that we can make sure we both understand?"

8. You shall not give false testimony against your neighbor.

God hates a lying tongue (Proverbs 6:17). Lying includes omitting information, withholding information, twisting the truth, telling white lies, and stating outright falsehoods with the purpose of deceiving another.[19] There is an enormous temptation to be secretive about our online activities when we know others might disapprove. My children and I have been guilty of this. Once I was dawdling online, scrolling through Hollywood gossip, then hastily switched windows when my boss walked around the corner.

We might tell our children, "God's standard is for us to always speak the truth. I have not lived up to this standard. I have lied and am still tempted to lie at times. I've suddenly shut down my screen when someone else walked into the room. I'm tempted to be secretive about some things that I do. Do you ever struggle with that temptation, too? I want us all to strive to be truthful and aboveboard. If I find out that you are being dishonest or secretive about your online activities, you may lose that privilege until our trust is rebuilt. I want you to have as much freedom as possible online. You earn that freedom by being trustworthy. There will be times when I monitor and check up on your online activity to help you remain honest. This is probably annoying and frustrating for you. Feel free to tell me how you feel.

"Let's pray for each other. 'Lord, help us all to be honest. Protect us from the temptation to lie and be secretive. We cannot do this well without Your help. In Jesus's name, amen.'"

9. You shall not covet your neighbor's house.

10. You shall not covet your neighbor's wife or anything that belongs to your neighbor.

We will cover theses commandments together. *Covet* is an archaic term that needs further explanation and present-day application. The definition is not to simply want, admire, and desire. Merriam-Webster defines it as an inordinate appetite to possess what belongs to another. It involves a lust that, if entertained, will likely lead to lying, stealing, adultery, and even murder to obtain the object of the desire. It is a form of fantasizing that, if left unchecked, will lead to immoral action. God warns us to monitor and harness our thoughts because they significantly impact our emotions and behaviors.[20]

Smartphones and social media burden us with an overwhelming knowledge of everything from which we are excluded. Masochistically, we are lured into a form of voyeurism, observing and obsessing over others' looks, possessions, activities, and even conversations. Is it surprising that this omniscience leads to jealousy, covetousness, and bitterness? We are drawn to compare our lives with the highlight reels of others' posted online. We are inevitably disappointed with our drab realities when compared to others' apparently glamorous, glitzy lives.[21]

You might say to your children, "Whom do you admire online? Have you ever found yourself obsessing about them and what they have? Have you ever felt bitter or resentful about it? I've fallen into that trap, too. I have obsessed about other people's looks, their food, their possessions. It is okay for us to want things and admire people, but it can be dangerous when our want becomes obsession. God asks us to be careful with our thoughts, to notice them, and to take control over them. It isn't easy to do; we have to practice. Let's pray for each other, 'God, You promise that You will give us the desires of our hearts as we delight in You. Please protect our hearts from unholy desires and help us to be open with one another. In Jesus's name we pray. Amen.'"

It is our God-given responsibility to teach our children God's standards and to structure our homes to model and safeguard His way. There is a boatload of promises about all the blessings that will be unleashed upon us if we do so. We must accept that our children have the right to decide whose way they will follow. Let's admit that we have all engaged in some rebellion with our own freedom. Let us do our part now to influence them through teaching, modeling, confession, high expectations, open dialogue, and prayer.

CHAPTER 5

Access as Leverage

We live in a culture that not only promotes owning the latest and greatest devices but boasts about our children doing so. According to recent surveys, 50 percent of children between the ages of two and eight have their own mobile devices. A majority of children are allowed to independently choose what they watch, when, and for how long. Depending on family income level, up to 64 percent of children under eight years old have a television in their bedrooms. Almost one-quarter of children under eight use a mobile device at mealtime. Thirty-nine percent live in homes in which the television is left on all or most of the time.[1]

Once children are allowed to own, control, and have unlimited access to digital devices, parents voluntarily give up one of their most valuable and effective sources of leveraging power and motivation. Digital activity is a highly desirable privilege for our children, especially when their access to it is limited. When we are willing to leverage their desire and link their access to screens to our expectations, uncooperative children can miraculously transform into compliant children.

Kids only have access to digital technology through their parents' resources. These are one of the few things we can control. It is not a child's right to have screens and use them as desired. While our children are under our roof, it is most loving and respectful to allow them to decide if they want the privilege of cell phones, computers, TVs, and video games based on the attitudes and behavior they choose. Good behavior, a respectful attitude, and work completion pay well. "Kids, do the difficult, right thing first and you will reap rewards."

I started reading parenting books when I was pregnant with Henry—a kind of last-minute crash course as I faced the intimidating task of becoming a mother. *Boundaries* by Drs. Henry Cloud and John Townsend and *Parenting with Love and Logic* by Dr. Foster Cline and Jim Fay were the most impactful at that time. They taught me the principles that have guided the way I discipline my children ever since. My husband would tell you how well our children respond to my teaching and authority. I cannot take full credit because, left to my own devices, I am a pushover, people-pleasing, conflict avoider. Basically, I am a walking, talking recipe for parenting disaster. But all these principles I am sharing with you, when applied, even through very imperfect parents like me, produce incredible results.

Using access to privileges as leverage with my children protects my inner peace, without which I cannot parent well. It is a philosophy of applying the Serenity Prayer in the action of parental discipline: accepting what we cannot change (our children), harnessing supernatural courage to change the things we can (our responses and resources), and having the wisdom to know how to leverage our limited but significant parental power.

The beauty of leverage is that it allows us parents to avoid arguments, fights, and power struggles. Personally, it greatly enables me to maintain my self-control because my focus and energy are channeled into controlling myself, not my kids or my spouse. I hardly ever raise my voice with my children and very rarely lose control in anger when they will not comply. I certainly experience frustration and impatience, but almost never at unmanageable levels because of the efficacy of this philosophy. Leverage allows me to calmly acknowledge what I can and cannot control, and it leaves the responsibility with my children to make their choices. It is an imitation of God's design and manner of dealing with us, His children.

"Henry and Junie, please clean your rooms now."

"Okay, Mom," they both reply. Junie runs upstairs and begins tidying up her toys. Henry lollygags, playing racecars with whatever small objects are closest at hand. Henry's delay is a pattern that often plays out in response to our requests. I wish he complied right away. I know that if he does not mature past his procrastination, he will face many avoidable problems in life. This matters a great deal to me and my husband— much more than it matters to Henry right now. How can we make it important to him? How can we make it his problem and not our problem?

I could remind Henry five times, more agitated each time that I have to egg him on to get him to comply. I could yell at him. That sometimes jolts him out of his distraction. I could grab him by the shirt, drag him up the stairs and hold his hands, forcing him to pick up each toy off his carpet. But those options deplete my energy and patience and ramp up my irritability. They pull me out of my serenity, because those tactics are all attempts to control my son and force him to comply. Whenever we parents try to control what is outside of our sphere of power, we drain our batteries and end up crabby and edgy. And although angry parenting can produce short-term compliance, it tends to result in long-term rebellion, resentment, and broken parent-child relationships. It is not our job to control our children, and when we try to work outside of our job description, distress, arguments, and discord ensue. Henry has a character defect in this area. He can be absentminded and easily distracted. His pace rarely matches my preference. I don't like being angry, yelling, or forcing him to do things. But I have to do something, don't I? Ignoring and allowing his disobedience would not be healthy for either of us.

Rather than trying to cajole, remind, and push him, I can leverage the resources that he desires. And that almost always results in Henry's compliance. "Hmm, I notice that you haven't gone upstairs to clean your room yet. That's too bad. Feel free to join us for the family movie once you've done what I have asked." All my children love pretty much any screen activity. Their access to screens motivates them. As we get the movie started without Henry, he suddenly bounds up the stairs, tosses the toys in the bin, stacks his books, and is back downstairs in less than five minutes. Cleaning his room is not important to him; watching movies is. So I leveraged his access to the movie to spur him on to complete his undesirable chore. Screen leverage is not our only form of motivation, but it is the technique most often used. Without our direct intervention, a disorganized room remains the default. Admittedly, our ability and willingness to address the mess ebbs and flows. Ideally, he tidies his room on a weekly basis.

We keep a list of daily and weekly chores for our children. Their assignments become more complex with their age and skill level. Their tasks currently include keeping the kitchen dish soap refilled, managing the recycling, sweeping the floor around the dinner table, tidying their rooms, and cleaning the bathrooms. We reevaluate our expectations several times annually to update and add to the list. We also require a positive attitude, respect, and a calm voice. (I hate whiny voices, don't you? That high-pitched complaining is so agitating and draining.) But we cannot control our children's attitude and tone of voice. We would go crazy trying, and it would just result in more whining and tears. But we can control what we make available to our children. Obedient kids with a calm voice and positive attitude who have finished their chores are welcome to entertainment screen time.

Junie asks, "May I watch a show?" Henry requests, "May I play my football video game?" I reply, "You are welcome to do so after your chores are completed." Their response ranges from whining and complaining to swift compliance. The beauty of the system is that I do not need to force them to complete their chores. I really cannot control their actions to that level (nor do I want to). But I can control access to our screens. So if they reply, "Ugh! This is so unfair. I just did my chores yesterday! Why do I have to do them again? You are so mean," I am not pulled into an argument. I can empathize and leave them to their choice. "Yeah, this is aggravating, huh? I hope you choose wisely. I would like for you to be able to earn your screen time."

Henry struggles with math. He becomes frustrated quickly and ends up shutting down, slumped over his desk, unwilling to talk or do the next math problem. My husband and I have been brainstorming how we can help him. Henry loves to use my cell phone to research cars and football, so I decided to experiment with the leveraging principle.

Early one morning, he joined me in the kitchen asking, "May I use your phone for a Google search?"

"Sure, you are welcome to five minutes, after you've completed five math problems," I responded.

"What? I have to do math right now?"

"Oh, no, you definitely don't have to do any math right now. I only ask you to do this math if you want to use my phone. Whether or not you do it is entirely up to you."

Henry huffed, thought for a few minutes, and then opened up his math workbook. He completed the five problems without further complaint. Leveraging was working its magic! So I sweetened the deal. "Henz, if you do three more problems, you can have ten minutes." He completed the next level of math and looked up at me with triumph and pride. I handed over my phone and he happily scrolled through football photos for a glorious ten minutes.

I didn't make Henry do anything. I simply allowed him to choose whether to fulfill the math requirement in order to enjoy using my phone. He felt better about himself because of his accomplishment, and we avoided a power struggle.

A few days later, he asked permission to play his video game. "You are welcome to your video game after you've done fifteen minutes of math practice with me," I said. Again, he complained for a minute and then complied. We ended up laughing and enjoying doing homework together. He earned his video game. Happy mom, happy Henry.

Whenever Henry uses my phone, I set my alarm for the time upon which we have agreed. He must return the phone at the alarm bell with gratitude. I had to add "gratitude" to the requirement because before I did, he would return the phone complaining that he had not had enough time. I cannot force him to speak words of appreciation, but I can withhold the privilege of using my phone (or any other screen). Grateful, responsible kids are welcome to share my screens with me.

I like to experiment with this formula of offering my children a variety of challenges and rewards and observing the results. I don't expect that they will happily receive my invitations, but I'm often surprised by their zeal, willingness, and industriousness. Sitting at the breakfast table on a Saturday morning, I announced that a new challenge was available. Anyone who scrubbed the toilets would be welcome to watch an unscheduled movie with me. All three kids hopped up from the table and scrambled to gather the toilet-cleaning equipment. They proudly called me in to inspect their work fifteen minutes later. The clock had not even struck 9 a.m. at that point, and the toilets were sparkling. Soon after, we were cuddled up in the living room, laughing together over the cartoon they chose as their reward. Does this sound far-fetched, idealistic, and unrealistic? I would be skeptical myself, except that I see similar results with my children over and over.

Humans have a built-in, God-given drive to work, produce, and accomplish. That impulse must be nurtured in order to bear fruit. On the other hand, it can be undermined and even extinguished. Our parental responsibility includes providing challenging, rewarding tasks to develop our children's work instinct.

Children are not guaranteed to respond well, but they often do. The younger we begin these lessons, the better the results. Digital media is an extraordinary leveraging tool.

Our children have an insatiable appetite for it, and it can be fairly affordable for us to provide if we stay out of the "latest and greatest" competition. We parents can maintain control over screens if we realize our power and exert our authority. Too many parents are not aware of the power that can and should be harnessed through screens for their children's good. Admittedly, this approach does require quite a bit of effort and diligence on our part, but it pays dividends.

Common challenges in this area include thoughts like:

- I cannot tolerate my children's displeasure.
- My spouse isn't on board.
- Consequences don't affect my children.
- It's too late for my family.
- My children refuse to comply.
- My child needs his phone!

Tolerating Children's Displeasure

Can we allow our disobedient children to experience loss and discomfort as a result of their poor choices? I often struggle to stand firm. My compassion and empathy compel me to rescue them from the distressing deprivation they have brought upon themselves. Sometimes we are motivated by guilt over having been harsh, absent, abusive, or divorced parents. We try to rectify those wrongs by spoiling our children. However, if we continually liberate our children from their own negative consequences, we do them a grave disservice. And we'll all suffer the worse pain of watching them grow into immature, irresponsible adults facing expensive real-world consequences.[2]

A pattern of unhealthy deliverance from the repercussions of bad behavior guarantees that the bad behavior will reoccur. Hot-tempered people must pay the penalty. Proverbs tells us that if you rescue them once, you will have to do it again (Proverbs 19:19). Disobedient, disrespectful kids should lose access to digital privileges. In the long run, the punishment is a blessing to them, the family, and even society. Humble, respectful, obedient children are a life-giving delight. Parents have the most powerful role to play in helping them develop that character through the administration of loss.

Henry recently accused me of being "super harsh" when I stuck to the discipline plan. Folks, need I remind you that I'm a recovering people-pleasing conflict-avoider? One of the main motivations in life for me has been gaining and maintaining the approval of others. Historically, it has crushed me to have others upset or disappointed with me. Disapproval used to eat away at my soul. Based on my history, living by this parenting philosophy would be nearly impossible for me in my own strength.

But I am convinced that this approach is part of loving my children well. So, I mulled over Henry's accusation, then gave myself a little self-evaluation and pep talk. *Am I being super harsh? Hmm, I clearly laid out the expectations for my kids. My son knowingly chose disobedience. I respect him enough to grant him that freedom. I think highly enough of him that I will allow him to choose the consequence he knew in advance would befall him. I did not raise my voice. I did not react out of uncontrolled anger. Nope, that's not harsh. That is clear, consistent, and loving parenting. My son will be a better man for my treatment of him. His wife and employers will appreciate the fruit produced by this process.* Our children's angry reactions may lead us to second-guess our discipline and relent.

Our children will inevitably balk against this system, especially if we have to make a course correction from lax parenting. We will be called ugly names and compared to other easygoing parents of friends. Our children will be angry with us. Our resolve will be shaken. We will need the backing and encouragement of a supportive spouse or friend to be able to persevere through our children's upset.

I strongly recommend setting up a support team of at least two people—ideally, your spouse and another trusted friend—who can provide prayer, cheerleading, and emotional reinforcement when the going gets tough with your kids. If your spouse and friends do not fit this job description, consider accessing a New Life therapist through www.newlife.com, or joining my online parenting community and training program through www.dralicebenton.com.

Once you have your support team in place, request from them the following: "I'm going to make some changes in my parenting regarding screen time. I know I'll have to withstand my children's ire. Would you be willing to provide me with prayer support? Could I touch base with you occasionally for a morale boost?" Then proactively seek their help so you can stay strong.

Spousal Disagreement

If your spouse is not interested in participating, rest assured that your efforts alone will still produce results. Your success will likely influence your spouse to support and imitate you over time. That has been the case with my husband and me. He was uncertain about my approach in the beginning and expressed concerns that I can be too soft and quick to comfort, with the risk of babying the kids. He has a point; that is a vulnerability of mine. But as he has seen the benefits of the leverage philosophy play out, I have witnessed him enacting many of these same techniques.

We will address strategies for handling significant spousal differences in chapter 7. For now, focus on the principle that you can only control your own approach. You can kindly request that your spouse join you, but it does not work to nag, complain, or force. Modeling with a positive attitude has a better chance of convincing him or her to join you.

Children's Apathy

What do we do when our children are apathetic and apparently unaffected by rewards and consequences? Sometimes they respond to our leverage transactions with teeth-grinding indifference: "I don't care." We must be prepared to up the ante and persevere.

For instance, Junie lost her screen privileges after disobeying my time limit and then lying to cover it up. This girl loves watching shows, so I was expecting the loss to affect her. To my shock, it didn't seem to matter at all! She did not express any remorse or regret, and happily played without screens.

On day two of the consequence period, she lied again about an unrelated issue. So we moved into day three of no digital entertainment, and she still seemed unaffected. In a prayerful parental strategy meeting, my husband and I decided to up the ante.

"Junie, it's too bad that your disobedience and lying have resulted in you losing screen time. We still don't see you repenting or apologizing, so an added consequence due to your choice is the loss of dessert after dinner." We were prepared to have her spend time alone in a chair or in her bed without toys if this didn't do the trick. Thankfully, the added consequence broke through her resistance. She apologized and asked for another chance. Phew!

Stalemates can last for days with strong-willed children. We must get creative and hold firm past our children's stubborn resistance in order to help them make better choices. Why was the first consequence inadequate? It may be that our children do not value it as much as we thought, they truly are fine without it and don't miss it, or in their obstinacy they are acting as if the loss does not matter to them.

It's Too Late for Me

Perhaps you feel overwhelmed because you didn't know or weren't equipped to lay a foundation of authority when your children were young. Maybe they already have the latest smartphone, a television in their room, and an iPad. They consider themselves to be the sole owner and authority over this equipment. You might suspect they watch inappropriate content. You see the light from their screen into the wee hours of the morning. You wonder if they have accessed pornography. Allowing screen privileges that our children have not earned while avoiding discipline and consequences usually results in a strong sense of entitlement and ingratitude. If some or all of this description fits your children, lay down your fear and despair here, because it is never too late. There is always hope. You can rectify your wrongs and reset the system with your kids. Consider this approach:

"I realize I have made many mistakes as a parent. When it comes to your screens, I either don't say anything, or I nag you to use them less and to watch better content. I know it drives you crazy when I bug you about it. I'm even hypocritical at times because I spend too much time on my own screens. I have not protected you well enough. I realize that allowing you to have full access to your screens without restriction and allowing screens in your room overnight is not good for you or me. This setup isn't working, and as the parent, I am at fault. Would you please forgive me?

"We are going to discuss a few changes. I want your opinion and input. You may use your screens for entertainment (pre-approved by me or Dad) once you have completed your homework and chores and are displaying a respectful, grateful attitude. Together we'll pick a time by which the screens will be left with me each night. You'll be welcome to pick up your screens the next morning after I'm awake. We've realized it will be better for all of us if we do not have televisions and computers in the bedrooms, as we are all staying up too late. We want you to help us decide where to have them in the common areas. I'm sure these changes will be trying for all of us. What are your thoughts?

"We don't want to micromanage you. We want you to be completely in charge of your own screen use as soon as you show you are being trustworthy and respectful.

"As long as you are respecting this arrangement, you'll be welcome to use screens and continue to receive allowance. We'll take your opinion about what the consequences should be if you decide not to cooperate. It will involve limiting access to privileges. We don't want to take privileges away from you. You actually have the power over whether you lose privileges based on your behavior. Your respect and cooperation will result in ongoing and increasing privileges and freedom for you. What are you thinking, and how are you feeling about these changes? Can you see ways we could handle this better?" (This is likely to be a heated discussion, so be prepared to listen to your child through the structure of the Comfort Circle while maintaining your decision).

We recently invited Henry to name a potential consequence for himself if he broke a minor commitment that he made to finish an extra task. He told us that he should lose his digital entertainment for three days if he didn't finish the work by the specified time. This was much harsher than I would have suggested. But I chose to accept his suggestion, and he finished the work three minutes later.

When parents set an expectation, it must be accompanied with a clear consequence if the child disobeys. Empty threats without follow-through are disastrous. Expectations must include clear guidelines and consequences. It is best to put them into writing and have parents and children sign the agreement so that it can be reviewed. Do so regularly and enforce the consequences consistently. Children naturally push parental boundaries to find out whether we mean what we say. As soon as they realize we aren't likely to enforce the consequences, it's game on. So before the consequences are declared, make sure you are willing and able to enforce them.

Refusal to Comply

Here's a common scenario we hear from parents:

"We told our teen that she must turn her phone in to us by 10 p.m. each night, but she ignores our requirement. Most nights she is chatting and watching TikTok until 2 or 3 a.m. She keeps us up, and she can't wake up on time and is crabby the next day. It is driving us crazy! I tried to take her phone the other day. She wouldn't let go of it and ended up throwing a fit. We wrestled for it. Eventually I got it. It was ugly."

Do not enter a tug-of-war with your child. Rather, influence him or her through leverage to voluntarily give the phone to you. Manhandling the situation may win you the screen, as long as you have the physical capacity to dominate your children, but it will be ruinous in the long run. It teaches children that they cannot learn to control themselves and so must be controlled by a stronger person. It places us in a position of further trying to control them physically rather than controlling ourselves and our resources.

Moreover, we have heard too many woeful tales of the tables turning in a way that resulted in violence between parent and child. We have seen the police and Child Protective Services get involved in these situations, as well as the destruction of the parent/child relationship. My warning is dire because the ramifications can be catastrophic.

Instead, try the following: "Hmm, that is unfortunate that you won't give me your phone. I'll have to decide what privilege to restrict because of your disobedience. Try not to worry about it." Leave the phone in their hand until they turn it in.

Now, increase their motivation by limiting access to the things over which you have control. Consider placing their cell phone plan on hold. If their stubbornness continues, be prepared to limit their access to other resources, screens, car rides, money, etc., until they relent. If your child is strong-willed, brace yourself through your peer support to wait them out as long as it takes, because their character and obedience are on the line. Let your actions speak louder than your words. Refrain from reminding, nagging, and trying to convince them; let leverage do the work.

Children Must Have a Cell Phone

Parents worry, "I cannot take my child's phone. She needs it to do homework and to stay connected with her friends. I need to be able to text her when I pick up her from school so I can find her. I need to be able to track her location on Find My Friends." It will be inconvenient for you and your child to make her surrender her phone. She will have to find other ways to access her online work and buddies.

Although it may seem as if we could not function without a cell phone, let us not forget that through the 1980s and '90s, most of us operated without them.[3] I didn't have my own cell until after college in 2003. I didn't have a smartphone until

2015. We all survived without them. Consider that the inconvenience pays dividends in character. Meting out discipline always comes at a price. We parents have to stand firm in the face of whining, crying, threats, tantrums, and whatever else our children throw at us. If we relent just because they are upset, the battle is lost.

Put the responsibility for the inconvenience this causes you back on the child. "Now that I can't text you at pickup time, I'll need you to be at our planned location at the designated time. Being responsible with this is part of the process of earning your phone back. And now that I cannot track you on GPS, I'll need you to check in once every hour that you are away after school to let me know where you are. You will have to ask to use your friend's phone to check in with me. You may have to talk with your teacher about accessing your online work another way. Your efforts will show me that I can trust you to have the phone back. I hope you choose wisely."

Do not be pulled into incorrectly assuming that your teen will be harmed by losing the phone. Will the loss hurt them? I sure hope so! Discipline is supposed to hurt. But when applied correctly, it does not harm. I define hurt as the temporary discomfort felt through the healthy consequence. Harm is long-term damage from mistreatment. The hurt, inconvenience, and annoyance are the secret sauce of discipline that, if mixed in at the correct measurements at the right frequency, culminate in behavior rectification. "No discipline seems pleasant at the time, but painful. Later on, however, it produces a harvest of righteousness and peace for those who have been trained by it" (Hebrews 12:11). John Townsend says, "We do not change until the pain of staying the same is greater than the pain of changing." Parents have to add in that disciplinary pain in order to motivate children to choose to change.

These leverage principles help us keep our parental heads cool. They also combine well with the Mentor and authoritative parenting styles previously discussed. We don't have to tussle with our children. We don't have to raise our voices. We don't have to control them. We simply declare our expectations, request their compliance, and dole out rewards or consequences accordingly—controlling ourselves and our resources, not our children. Of course, we won't apply this philosophy perfectly. We don't always have the energy and drive to maintain the structure. Some days the chores are left undone and the kids are allowed unmerited access to digital entertainment.

Our children can also be so aggravating and persistent in their requests that we are tempted to give them the unearned screen access to stop their whining. It is simple, easily justifiable, and it efficiently keeps them entertained. Is it really such a big deal if we allow them a few hours of unmerited digital diversion? When we parents hit exhaustion, their digital amusement can provide us a much-needed break. However, the goal of developing a respectful young adult who is trustworthy with screens is built through regular investment to maintain discipline. We don't have to be perfect. But the more consistent we are with our expectations and requirements, the better the chance of raising responsible, grateful children.

Let's try our best, notice our failures, and work to succeed more and fail better the next time. Be patient with yourself, your spouse, and this process. Your family will be better off as you apply this philosophy. Your children's future relationships, employers, and even society will reap the benefits.

CHAPTER 6

Focusing on What Is Pure

Our digital diet affects our well-being. It can nourish and replenish our emotional and spiritual reserves or decrease and deplete them. The default mode is to be a passive consumer, allowing the world to choose what it wants to pour into our eyes and ears. Our culture celebrates and pushes content that includes violence, horror, and sex—even to our young children.

Do you regularly evaluate and question what you and your kids consume and whether it benefits you? Digital wariness is an invaluable lesson to model and impart to our children, but most of us have become digitally numb. Why has it become the norm for us to allow harmful material to flood into our homes through our screens? We are bombarded by images and information that threaten to destabilize our internal peace. Do we count the cost of our entertainment?

What should our expectations be? Serenity is best maintained when we intentionally focus on things that are true, noble, right, pure, lovely, admirable, and praiseworthy (Philippians 4:8). How much of your content meets those criteria these days? Do you have the courage to call yourself and your family to a healthier standard?

Digital activity and content can be broken down into four categories:

- **Enriching:** This kind of digital media is clean. It facilitates growth, health, and contentedness in the long term. It usually increases knowledge and wisdom. This is the veggie, fruit, and protein of the digital diet. It includes wholesome shows, video games, and influencers who are inspiring and uplifting.
- **Neutral:** This material is nondetrimental entertainment that can bring levity and laughter and allow a soothing escape from reality. It is not necessarily growth-oriented. This is the cheeseburger and brownie at the end of a long day. A

good meal plan includes some comfort food and dessert.

- **Vapid:** This content is mindlessly entertaining. It often involves gossip and questionable material. This is the Twinkie of the diet. Its harm may not be significant in small doses, but too much will be.
- **Pernicious:** This type of digital media is harmful and evil to varying degrees. This is the hemlock and the rat poison of the diet. It leads to spiritual, emotional, and relational death over time.

Ideally, the majority of our family's digital diet will be Enriching with some Neutral content. Vapid and Pernicious content is best avoided, but is admittedly the most alluring and titillating. Of course, there is often overlap between categories. How can we make sure that Enriching and Neutral content fills our children's digital diets?

We should regularly seek out new Enriching options to offer our children, such as streaming programs, apps, and digital games using clean subject matter that promotes our family values.

Our family has researched and tried a few companies like Pure Flix, Yippee, and Minno that stream cartoons and movies.

These are all subscription-based programs that are reasonably priced and are tailored to particular age groups and faiths. We are currently using Minno, which is aimed at elementary-aged children.

It felt risky to present Minno to my kids. I wondered how much they might balk at the conversion from secular, popular shows with high-production budgets to faith-based programs with obviously smaller production budgets. I was yet again surprised by and grateful for their enthusiastic reception. Granted, my kids are nine years old and under. Attempting this transition in the teenage years would meet with more resistance.

My kiddos' current favorite cartoon is *Bibleman*, in which a team fights villains and evil with Scripture. I would never have guessed that would be their top choice. But I was again reminded that when I am enthusiastic and upbeat (despite my uncertainty), my children usually buy in and follow suit. My heart and conscience are much more at ease when they are watching programs that I can trust and know to be Enriching and free of commercials.

When it comes to online games, we use several educational programs like Lightgliders, ABCmouse, Blooket, and Reading Eggs. They teach reading, math, history, and science through fun games. My son can go from a frustrating math class at school to voluntarily undertaking math challenges in Reading

Eggs minutes later. My children often ask to play these programs as soon as they wake up and as soon as school is over. I feel comfortable and confident allowing them to spend some time this way each day. They recently asked me to join them in Lightgliders, urging me to set up my own avatar. We were all cuddled on the same couch, each with a screen, teaming up against the bad guys. It was a blast, and it allowed me a foot into their world! I would never have joined in without being motivated by the material herein. My children are still young enough to desire my company. Their invitations have an expiration date. But it can still be difficult to choose to join them in their digital world, which is outside of my comfort zone. We parents need to respond to these bids for attention. The invitation will not remain open forever.

We also use Epic and TumbleBooks, which provide access to e-books and read-alouds for young children. Facilitating my children's reading is one of my highest priorities. My daughter could spend hours using this app.

Benton family video games currently include baseball, racing, football, *Minecraft*, *LittleBigPlanet*, and *The Bible Game*. We use them as time to play together and discourage our children from playing alone.

Providing, encouraging, and participating with our children in Enriching programming increases the likelihood that they will choose and enjoy it for themselves. This is not guaranteed, but it is something we have the power to influence. It is also Mentor parenting.

The flip side of this coin is limiting and eliminating the Vapid and Pernicious content. What do you need to remove from your digital diet? It always works best to clean our side of the street first. Personally, I had to eliminate romances with sex scenes, zombie gore, and Hollywood gossip. (That last one is still a guilty pleasure that I have to work to avoid.)

Early in my marriage, before we had children, my husband and I became engrossed in an apocalyptic zombie show. The storyline was engaging and suspenseful. The scenes were violent and grotesque. It was awful and captivating. We watched the show with another couple from work. It was fun talking over the most recent episode and guessing what was to come. At times, we got together to watch the show and have a meal. Every week, we all looked forward to the next creepy installment of the tale. We bonded over the show and felt a sense of belonging through our shared experience.

Being scared and even horrified can be thrilling. More graphic, realistic, and even sadistic content results in magnified relief once the tension is resolved. The period of unpleasant pain amplifies the subsequent pleasure.[1] Intentionally scaring someone else feels powerful. Younger siblings often tell tales of being traumatized by frightening content that gleeful older siblings force on them.

Researchers have studied the long-term effects of exposure to fear-inducing digital content.[2] Ninety percent of people surveyed were able to recall in detail frightening content they had viewed decades ago. A quarter indicated that they still experienced some related ongoing anxiety. Half of those interviewed reported that the spooky material had precipitated both sleeping and eating disturbances in childhood. The earlier the age of exposure, the stronger the effect on the child.[3]

The majority of participants indicated that the frightening show was chosen by someone else, and that they watched it with others in the evening. The stimuli that resulted in the most prolonged anxiety included blood, injections, or injury and disturbing sounds or distorted images. Many participants revealed that they continued to struggle with fear and disturbed sleep, and avoided similar situations for months and even years afterward. Exposing children to unnecessary levels of fearful material results in a panoply of long-lasting symptoms and behaviors that are "a nuisance to parents and a burden to children."[4]

What movie most frightened you as a child? I'll bet you have an immediate answer with an accompanying flashback. My memory is a mere moment from an old black-and-white

Dracula movie when a detective enters a dark room alone. Suddenly, a female vampire pops up into a sitting position from her coffin. That vampire used to haunt me, even into early adulthood.

In my childhood home, there was a small kitchenette and bedroom in our basement for guests. We stored our extra milk in the fridge there, and my mom often would send me downstairs alone to bring a carton up for dinner. Basements can be pretty gloomy on Minnesota winter nights. I would run down, grab the milk, and race back up without looking at that dark corner of the room. I was terrified that the vampire lady would be lying in the bed in the shadows. I was a quiet kid and didn't voice my fears. My parents were very protective of us when it came to sexual content, but they were not as sensitive to how potent scary content can be for young minds.

Not until I was in my early thirties did I realize how much I am negatively impacted by frightening and gory images. I was experiencing an uncomfortable amount of anxiety, insomnia, and irritability at the time, so I evaluated the things in my life that were exacerbating my emotional discomfort. Remember that apocalyptic zombie show? Although it was fun watching in the moment, it dawned on me that it was burdening my spirit! I made the surprisingly difficult choice to stop watching it.

I was afraid to tell our little group of my decision, feeling foolish, childish, and worried about their ridicule. To my surprise, they accepted my decision with curiosity and understanding. The ongoing choice to avoid the show and miss out on the fun was trying. But I paid a higher price to watch it than I did in refraining from watching it. That one change made a big difference in my anxiety and insomnia, and I started feeling better quickly.

Think of the strong influence of peer groups, for good or bad. If it is difficult for us as adults to abstain from an activity popular with our peers, how much more challenging is it for our children?

I abhor being the annoying, goody-two-shoes, overly sensitive naysayer. But I operate best when my internal serenity is well guarded. My children are better off when I protect their emotional and spiritual peace. Zombie shows do not bless me. Dark content burdens my family. So, through many cringe-inducing moments, I have chosen to speak up when I see content that will be disturbing for us. My go-to phrases have become: "Oh boy, that doesn't work for me. I need to fast-forward through this. I need to turn this off. This movie isn't good for us."

At first, I felt as if I were the only person in the room whose radar was alerted to potential—sometimes obscure—spiritual and emotional digital danger. I battle a critical voice in my own head that chides, "Come on, settle down. This is just a fun fantasy kids' movie. Why do you have to be so uptight?" I have to pray and cheer for myself in these moments. "God, You gave me the job of protecting and guiding my children. I don't want to be the naysayer. But this doesn't feel right. Help me to have a voice of opposition even if everyone is upset with me for it." This is a slowly developing muscle. It is never comfortable to be the one exercising it. Nonetheless, I would much rather be erroneously overprotective than underprotective when it comes to my children's digital diets.

There were a few times early on when my husband seemed mildly annoyed with my concern. But over our nine years of parenting together, I have seen his radar and mine become more finely tuned. As I have spoken up, he has become more sensitive to what material may be inappropriate for our children. Sometimes, he even speaks up before I do. Generally, he now agrees quickly with my concerns. I feel protected and well covered by my husband when he turns off a movie, explaining to our children why the content is not acceptable for us. Dads, we need your protection of our sensitive hearts and minds, even when we don't know it and when we fight against it.

I grew up enjoying magical fantasy cartoons and movies. You probably did, too. Content geared toward children is saturated with magic. Psychic shows are very popular. Ghost shows are fascinating. Witchcraft is making a comeback with our youth. I'm intrigued by all of it.

But did you know that God warns us, "Let no one be found among you who sacrifices their son or daughter in the fire, who practices divination or sorcery, interprets omens, engages in witchcraft, or casts spells, or who is a medium or spiritist or who consults the dead. Anyone who does these things is detestable to the Lord" (Deuteronomy 18:10–12)? I don't like this biblical expectation and feel ill-equipped to take a stand against everything listed here. Most magic seems like harmless fairytale fodder to me. But I trust that God's rules are in the best interest of my family, so I pray that He makes me more sensitive to this material and bolder in curtailing it in my home.

We tried watching *The Princess and the Frog*, a G-rated children's cartoon released in 2009. Our family had settled in, popcorn bowls in hand. We were enjoying the delightful New Orleans music and the heroine's work ethic and determination. We had a rude awakening when a character used voodoo to communicate with his "friends on the other side." Creepy, shadowy figures appeared to do his will and undermine the hero and heroine of the tale. They seemed to be either spirits of the dead or demons. I pushed past my conflict avoidance and people-pleasing to ask my husband to turn off the movie, telling my children that watching voodoo and evil spirits isn't good for us. I thought they would all be annoyed with me for being "overly sensitive." To my surprise, my husband fully agreed and my children were relieved. It was too scary for them. And yet, I suspect that if I had kept my concern quiet, we would have watched the whole movie. Folks, who will speak up?

I did not grow up with cable television and was truly only exposed to it in any significant amount during my relationship with my husband in my late twenties. At the time, I was taken aback by the repetitiveness, violence, and sexual content of commercials that accompany normal programming, but I soon grew accustomed to it. Before I became a parent, my radar didn't compel me to turn it off, but my awareness has sharpened as I have watched my children watch and as I have practiced applying biblical standards.

Imagine hearing your spouse say, "Whoa, this commercial isn't good for our kids. Let's not leave them in the living room alone with the TV on!" That sounds unhinged even to me! Nonetheless, commercials are another area in which I have had to develop my sensitivity and my assertiveness. I am determined to take as much holy authority as I can over what our screen is allowed to show us.

We commonly have a football game or golf tournament playing on TV on the weekends. The adults move in and out of the room as we do chores and prep meals. Sports are harmless content, right? Our kids are fine for a few minutes alone in front of the TV...right?

But one of the first commercials that sounded the alarm for us played during a golf tournament. The spot begins with live-action golfers and commentators speaking in hushed tones. Enormous massive tentacles suddenly shoot out of a pond on the golf course and grab the golfer and his caddy, sweeping multiple bystanders off their feet and into the water. The commentators' tone doesn't change in the least as they remark on the appearance of the sea monster snatching up human beings. The narrator points out that if you are a commentator, you whisper. If you want to save 15 percent on insurance, you get that brand. My son, who was five at the time, was in the living room racing his cars as the commercial played. He didn't seem to be paying attention to the screen. However, at 3 a.m. he awoke, sobbing that a monster was grabbing him. I didn't realize the connection until I saw the commercial play again the next weekend. From a child's perspective, the advertisement is reality television. In thirty seconds, that image was burned into my child's brain and later turned into a nightmare.

It is altogether too easy and common to dismiss our children's fearful reactions. Your own parents may have told you, "Come on, that isn't even real. Don't be scared. It's no big deal." They may have even laughed at your fear. But children's fear is a big deal that should be taken seriously by the adults assigned to protect them. What goes into our children's ears and eyes can affect their hearts, minds, and souls for a lifetime.

Let us also be wary of sexual content slipped into and around sporting events on television. Despite not being a big football fan, even I get excited about the Super Bowl, the halftime show, and the much-anticipated commercials. To my chagrin, the content sometimes borders on pornography. The "family-friendly" Super Bowl includes halftime shows with a concerning amount of sexualized dancing, lyrics, and up-close camera shots of women's breasts and crotches. I have felt disturbed, but again second-guessed my reaction. "Am I just being a killjoy?"

The world has always tried to pull our sons into objectifying women and has tried to teach our daughters that sex appeal is their greatest asset and should be flaunted. Let us not stand idly by and allow this to go unchecked on our watch, in our own living rooms!

What are you and your children watching during individual, isolated screen time that depletes rather than nourishes your spirit? Are you willing to explore the dark content that attracts your children? In my experience, plenty of young people are surprisingly willing to discuss their digital habits, as if they have been waiting and hoping someone would show interest. Some readily divulge what they are consuming, how often, and for how long. I have frequently been told, "No one has ever asked me before."

We may be hesitant to invade our children's privacy. However, too much privacy is dangerous, increasing the chance that our children will be victimized. Our kids may respond with agitation and annoyance to our questions and interference, but I also have heard expressions of relief and gratitude from children whose parents stepped up their digital involvement, monitoring, and protection.

I purposefully do sporadic spot checks to monitor the content of my kids' shows and games, which they are only welcome to play in communal areas, not their bedrooms. Any show or game can be stricken from our approved list. If our children watch it again against our wishes, they lose screen privilege until they rebuild the trust. Trust is rebuilt through a display of repentance, an apology, acceptance of their consequence, and additional chores.

If you are willing to check and ask, be prepared to discover the good and the bad. I have come across children as young as seven years old playing bloody, brutal, horrific video games for hours. Children have reported that they spend half the day in their rooms watching YouTube videos celebrating aberrant sexual behavior. I have heard from kids under ten years old who have been contacted online by Momo, a ghastly figure with a woman's head and a bird's body. Momo invites them to play a game involving increasingly risky challenges. It eventually tells them to kill themselves, threatening that if they do not comply, their parents and siblings will be harmed. All these things had been taking place for some time, unbeknownst to the children's parents—who were often only feet away! These young people told me just because I asked with a noncritical voice of warmth and concern.

Why might dark content appeal to our children? We all have some level of morbid curiosity. There is a genetic propensity in some children, especially adolescent boys, to be sensation seekers.[5] They seem to have the inborn makings of hunters and warriors, a desire to take on dangerous missions. They tend to be attracted to thrill and adventure, desire novel experiences, and are uninhibited and easily bored.[6] Sensation seekers enjoy aggressive play, live and digital. Violent video games can become an outlet for their natural bent for aggression. Violent games, played repeatedly, increase one's tolerance and decrease sensitivity in a way that often leads the player to seek more extreme content in order to achieve the same thrill previously experienced.

Trauma survivors report that horror videos and games that contain aspects of their own traumatic experiences can both trigger their painful memories and at the same time give them a sense of control. Some video games such as *Dead by Daylight*, *Friday the 13th*, and *Resident Evil: Resistance* allow a player to take the role of the villain and engage in evil deeds, including graphic torture and murder. Some youth report that they enjoy perpetrating digital violence and wish they could also do so in real life! The thoughts and behaviors that we rehearse online are likely to become what we think, feel, and do in real life.[7]

All these children would fare better if their parents were warmly curious and willing to monitor their digital activity. Parental warmth and supervision have been shown to significantly reduce the chances of children developing addictive behavior, substance use, and delinquent behavior online and offline.[8]

Do you remember when your children were toddlers? When they were out of your sight and quiet for too long, your alarm bells went off. Their prolonged silence was never a good thing. You would seek them out and find them dumping flour all over the kitchen floor, cutting their sister's hair, or using your lipstick as body paint. The need for supervision does not end at preschool. When our adolescents and teens are too quiet for too long, it is a warning sign that we need to check on them. But let's not wait for it to be too late. Let's make friendly, loving, nosy check-ins the norm rather than the exception. Even as adults, we make wiser choices when we are checked on or when we intentionally check in with caring peers. Accountability, annoying though it may be, blesses us.

So start asking your children in a gentle, noncritical voice, "What are you interested in lately online and on TV? What are your favorite shows? Who are your favorite influencers? What attracts you to them? Are you into any horror shows? What games do you enjoy playing?" Then respond through the structure of the Comfort Circle: listen, reflect, and invite more information.

Notice your internal reactions to your child's responses. Do you feel pleasure, relief, fear, criticism, or disgust? Can you restrain your negative reaction temporarily? Can you intentionally remain curious as to why your child would be drawn to these digital activities? Withhold your natural urge to react quickly, possibly with anger and discipline. Find out what attracts your child to that content and how it was introduced to them. You will then be better equipped and will have more relational equity to effectively respond.

This gentle, persistent curiosity and engagement does not mean that we accept and cosign our child's unhealthy pursuits. It just means that we stay inquisitive longer than is comfortable so that our response is measured, effective, and targeted to the real problem.

If we react too quickly out of emotional discomfort, we might miss the discovery of hidden hurt and confusion taking place inside our child who is yearning to be known and loved and has probably felt overlooked and unimportant. I recommend researching their answers before responding to them. Gather information with your spouse, pray over your discovery, and then decide on a course of action. Optional responses include:

- I looked into the show you told me about. I can see how it could hold your interest. How did you find out about it? How long have you been watching it? Do you notice if you ever feel anxious or down after watching it? How do you think it lines up with our Christian values? I noticed that it involves _____, which goes against our beliefs. For your sake, I need to ask you to stop watching it. I know that can be very hard to do. What do you think? Are you willing to stop?

- If your child resists: I hear that you aren't willing to stop. That's too bad. If you choose not to comply, I will have to consider what action I will take. I cannot support you watching this.
- Follow up with a prayerful consequence such as loss of screen privileges, administered with more warmth and loving concern.

By leaning in to their digital worlds, we can learn a great deal about our children. Our inquisitiveness will lead us to discover surprising and possibly concerning behavior, hidden hurts, and trauma. Armed with that knowledge, we can much more effectively understand and love our young folk. We can increase protective structure while treating the roots below the behavior.

CHAPTER 7

Parental Disagreement

What should you do if your spouse's digital standards are drastically different from your own? Is this a battle worth fighting? Well, it depends on how you fight. Ongoing, heated parental conflict takes a major toll on children from infancy to adulthood. If your conversations about screens include raised voices, condescension, insults, name-calling, physical aggression, door slamming, or threats of leaving or divorcing, you are hurting your marriage and your children even as you try to protect them.[1] But if you address this issue with humility, confession, gentle requests, grace, mercy, understanding, truth, praise, encouragement, and prayer, then you are fighting in a worthy, holy, and effective way. In most conversations, we would do well to remember Ben Franklin's adage: tart words make no friends; a spoonful of honey will catch more flies than a gallon of vinegar. Let's learn how to have grace-filled conversations about digital differences using God's weapons of warfare.

When I was dating, digital behavior was not on my list of priories. My husband-to-be enjoyed television as regular evening entertainment. We had great fun watching shows in his bachelor pad. This detour from my no-television life was enjoyable for several years.

But having babies changed my priorities and ramped up my protective instincts. Objectively, I pulled an unexpected, unfair, 180-degree shift in several areas of life, including my practice of faith, screens, alcohol consumption, and cigarette smoking. So who owes the first apology? I'm the one who tried to change the rules of the game.

Several years ago, we combined households with my husband's mother. In the early days of our multigenerational home, the television was often on. My mother-in-law enjoys background television noise in her room throughout the day, staying on top of current events. She loves to connect with her grandchildren by bringing them online with her. She likes to have them all cuddled on her bed to watch cartoons together. She founded the Turtle Club, a cross-country video conference to teach the grandchildren about sea life, and brings in extended family members to make presentations about different sea creatures. My stay-at-home husband is glad to give the kids an after-school cartoon break. Remember my old belief that not having a television is better for kids? My anxiety skyrocketed over our digital differences!

Rather than calmly addressing our discrepancies, I went into fear-and-control mode. I would walk into the room, see the kids watching cartoons with either my husband or mother-in-law, abruptly turn off the television, and have the kids come outside to play with me. Tension steadily mounted! It took me several months and many therapy sessions to be able to broach the topic with my family. I was afraid to voice my desires, imagining my wishes would be rejected.

One night at dinner, with much trepidation, I asked my husband and mother-in-law if they would be willing to consider a request. Would they please join me in restricting screen time for the kids to one to two hours per day? I withheld my true desire of only weekend television or no television, knowing that would go over like a lead balloon.

Given my passive-aggressive approach up to that point, my request was understandably met with some resistance. My mother-in-law pointed out that screen time was one of her preferred activities with her grandchildren, and my request would curtail her ability to engage with the kids and limit her own personal leisure time. She also pointed out how agitating it had been for her that I would rudely turn off the television she had been watching with the kids. She was right. My husband pointed out that he was the stay-at-home parent and had the lion's share of dealing with the kids, and my request would make his job much more difficult. He was right.

The temperature in that room rose quickly for me. I tried to listen through the Comfort Circle steps, to understand and acknowledge their concern, but we were all getting stirred up and I quickly reached my listening limit. I told them that I needed to step away from the conversation and I would revisit it later. I was shell-shocked and felt alone in my concern. I was completely taken aback by their reaction. It ranks as one of the most distressing family conversations I've ever had. It felt like my authority as a mother was being bypassed in an area of parenting that is really important to me.

I eventually came to understand that my methods had been disrespectful to my family, and I knew I needed to address my behavior with them. Taking a humble and curious posture would give the best chance of us all softening toward one another, gaining understanding, and possibly reaching a compromise. I had repair work to do. So I set aside my rebuffed feelings and asked God for the supernatural ability to listen first, without expressing my own hurt.

I sought out my husband, offering to listen to him through the Comfort Circle. I was able to see that my desire could, and very likely would, make his job more difficult, especially in the short term. I had the unfair advantage of being raised by a mother who had modeled what I hoped to have in my home. Television isn't meaningful to me, so it is easy for me to go without it. I was asking him to change lifelong habits in the context of his demanding 24/7 job of being the primary caregiver to our children. The television is such an effective pacifier that it was tough for him to imagine limiting it to just two hours through his never-ending days of childcare. I think it felt like I was saying, "Now that we've been married for a few years, I suddenly need you to be drastically different in your digital behavior than you have been your whole life. I want you to work twenty-four-hour shifts with the kids for the next eighteen years. You can only take a two-hour TV break per shift." My request was much bigger than I could have imagined, but after I thoroughly listened and validated his reaction, he agreed to try to limit screen time! I gratefully accepted his willingness and didn't push my luck for a larger commitment.

I then privately went to my mother-in-law and asked to listen to and reflect on her concerns. She loves her grandkids and enjoys her time with them. In my request, she had basically heard, "Grandma, I need you to cut your own screen time from as much time as you want down to two hours. We are going to limit the kids' screen time, so they will not be allowed to spend the time with you that you would like, in the way you feel comfortable. So please shut off your TV in your own room once you've reached your two-hour max and send the kids out." That was the message she had heard from me.

It would be natural for me to push back and retort, "That's not what I said!" But explaining my stance and defending myself at this point in our conversation would not bring us toward reconciliation. Arguing polarizes us, and we all dig our heels in even more. Humility, listening, reflecting, and validating another's experience brings harmony and gives the best chance for a compromise. Those are God's weapons, and they often win the skirmishes.

I acknowledged that my request, delivery, and behavior had negatively affected them. I asked for their forgiveness. This exchange brought the temperature back down. We all eventually agreed that the kids would have to earn their cartoon time by finishing chores and homework. They had to always ask permission from Mom or Dad, even if they wanted to watch Grandma's television.

Despite his initial hesitation, my husband has often ended up limiting their digital entertainment to even less than two hours per day. Grandma has the kids work on art projects in her room. She recently had all three building miniature fairy gardens, and she spurs them on to regular garden maintenance.

I will always prefer attracting my children to nonscreen activities. But through writing this book, God has challenged my superiority and self-righteousness. And to my surprise, it turns out my approach was not the best. I was a Limiter who needed to loosen up into a Mentor. My husband and mother-in-law had been doing so much more digital mentoring than I had!

I try to notice when my husband and mother-in-law do alternate activities with the kids and praise them for it. I also look for the positive in their screen engagement. Grandma's screen time is frequently educational, and it is her way of building relationship with them and babysitting them, giving us a break. I can still feel tension and some anxiety when I think the kids have had too much screen time. When that's the case, I get them playing something else as soon as I'm available. I do what I can and try to accept and release what is out of my control. We may always disagree to some extent. With God's grace, we can love each other through our differences.

We must factor in the importance of protecting relationship as primary over the secondary good of managing screen time. Allowing more digital entertainment than I want benefits the relationships in my family. I needed to loosen up. Do you?

We do not control the other adults in our home and in our children's lives, nor should we try. Let's learn from my mistakes. If they do not agree with your digital approach, I suggest the following:

1. Take your differences into prayer first, asking for the wisdom that God promises (James 1:5). Prayer slows down our reactivity and reassures us that we are not acting alone. "Lord, I want our family to follow Your divine design. Please show me where I am wrong in my belief and my approach. Inspire me and my spouse to align with Your will when it comes to our screens. Help us both to be submissive to You and to one another. Show me any areas in which I am falling short, particularly if I have been critical or nagging toward my spouse about screens. Lead us in Your way everlasting."

2. If you have disagreed, you probably have criticized, and most of us don't do that with grace and a gentle tone. Your willingness to see where you were imperfect, hurtful, or just plain annoying will actually serve you very well in your overall purpose. Bring that realization into a confession.

3. Remember that removing the beam from your own eye first always brings grace and softens your spouse to hear your request. You might say, "I want to confess that I have been complaining and nagging you about the kids' screen time. I bet you have felt attacked. I see that I haven't had a great approach in talking about screens. And I have drastically altered my stance from our lives, pre-children. I've expected to you be fully on board with me. I've gotten angry with you, called you names, and raised my voice. I should have handled that better. Would you tell me how it has affected you?" Listen in the Comfort Circle style. Ask for forgiveness.

4. Pick your battles. If your spouse is strongly opposed or defensive, make your request small and doable. Do not lay blame on your spouse. Accusations are not beneficial here. Take personal responsibility. "I want to establish some new expectations for our kids. Could I share one with you? I realize that I have let the kids spend too much time alone on their screens. Would you consider both of us carving out a little time this week to play a game with the kids online or offline?

What would you like to do with them? How can I help set it up?"

Your spouse might receive the following suggestions better if you address them one at a time spread out over several weeks. In my opinion, these are the most important changes to make:

- Increase online and offline joint family activities.
- Intentionally accessing Pernicious content will result in a loss of digital privileges.
- One meal per day includes a parent (ideally Dad) leading a brief devotional and discussion questions.
- Meals are screen-free.
- Parents will check on digital activity regularly.
- Screens off before bedtime.
- Children may use screens in common areas only. If this is a drastic change for your family, wait to address it. Work on the other changes first for several weeks.

If our desires are preferences rather than moral or ethical God-given mandates, we should consider applying the unpopular submission principle where possible, "Submit to one another out of reverence for Christ" (Ephesians 5:21). For instance, my husband can spend hours watching sports on the weekend. It is more than I want my children to watch. But I don't think my preference is morally superior. In fact, I see the relational engagement between my husband and sons in this arena. So I submit to his preference and don't complain about it. Conversely, my husband thinks I am overly protective of our children regarding some digital material, but he submits to my preference.

When I believe my preference is in the best spiritual interest of our children, I will hold my ground and pursue my belief, such as not allowing Pernicious content.

Here are a few more ideas:

1. If your spouse completely disagrees with any of the requests: "Thank you for hearing me out. Would you explain why you disagree?" Listen in the Comfort Circle style. "Is there anything I could do to help you consider what I'm asking? I'm sad that you don't agree. I'm going to do what I can to enact these ideas. Would you please think and pray about my request? I will need to check

back with you about this. Would you like me to bring it up in one week or two?"

2. Take your spouse's disagreement and your frustration to prayer and a trusted peer. Prayer is God's mighty, behind-the-scenes difference maker. Do not underestimate its power. "God, my spouse keeps letting me down. I feel like I'm alone in this battle. I'm frustrated, resentful, and worn out. Help me to move toward forgiving my spouse. I choose to pray a blessing over him in obedience to You. Please change his mind and help him to see how the kids and I need him to protect us and model how to use screens responsibly. I cannot do this without You. I trust You. Thank You in advance for what You are and will be doing. In Jesus's name I pray. Amen."

3. Refrain from addressing your concerns for the agreed-upon time. Any further pushing, nagging, or complaining will probably set your spouse against you even more. Avoid trying to argue your spouse into agreement. Parental conflict significantly impacts children, resulting in emotional distress, difficulty adjusting, and higher levels of depression and anxiety.[2] It would likely be more detrimental to

expose your children to ongoing heated arguments about screens than to the screens themselves. It will also pit your children against you as they align with the more lenient parent.

4. Praise, praise, and praise any positive change you notice in your spouse

CHAPTER 8

Building an Interesting Offscreen Life

Discovering God's purpose and pursuing it is one of the best routes to the most interesting and fulfilling life. It is also one of the quickest ways to increase genuine self-esteem. We were designed to complete fruitful work—and to enjoy the process. Even in the Garden of Eden, Adam and Eve had jobs to do. In our fallen world, work is laborious, but it can also be gratifying if our talents are matched with the correct training and level of challenge. We are to help our children discover their gifts and grow them into God's mission for their lives. Part of that discovery process includes enrolling them in real-life training so that they are ready to launch into the world. Some of this must take place on screens because we live in an increasingly digital world. But a good portion must take place offscreen, too, even if God is calling your child to be a video game developer or a social media expert. The training described in this chapter can teach our children how fascinating and rewarding life can be offscreen.

My parents used to tell us that when we were out of the house and they had an empty nest, they were off to see the world, so we should be prepared to fend for ourselves. They were going to sell their home, buy an RV, and travel the country sans children. It was mostly a joke and never happened, but the goal of being independent at eighteen excited and motivated us to pursue increasing self-sufficiency. It also gave us a sense of urgency—we had work to do to get ready to provide for ourselves.

In our relatively prosperous society, wealth fosters inactivity and low expectations for children. If you don't think you are wealthy, consider this: if you have any money in the bank, money in your wallet, and a container of spare change, then you are in the wealthiest 8 percent of people in the entire world, according to the Red Cross.[1]

Many American children do not need to work while in school. We have created environments in which they can solely focus on academics and extracurricular activities without the burden of an after-school job. What an amazing country we live in! I have worked with many immigrants from impoverished parts of South America who were taken out of elementary school out of necessity to work the fields or in factories to help feed their families. Many never returned to school or achieved literacy; some are still unable to sign their own names.

However, there is a downside to American prosperity. Our children often have too much downtime, which sucks them into hours of passive digital entertainment. Even though many of us do not need our children to work to pay our bills, they need to work for their own good. Our country is suffering from a weak work ethic in our younger generations.

Before 2020, adolescents were spending an average of 7.5 hours per day just on digital entertainment.[2] In 2020, 25 percent of youth ages fourteen to twenty-two reported that they were on social media almost constantly.[3] Children from one to eight years old were spending three to four and a half hours with digital media per day. Among children less than one year old, 47 percent were watching an average of two hours of shows per day.[4] All of those numbers have only increased since then, by as much as two to three hours per day.[5] Some of the increase in screen time was necessary as school moved online due to the COVID-19 pandemic. Our children were physically separated from their friends. Parents were becoming homeschool teachers.

We were juggling work, loss of work, and increased at-home childcare. Our children's increase in digital activity is likely to remain—if we allow it.

Does your child have too much downtime? Probably. Let's consider how we can put some of this time to good use. More than three-quarters of adults report that they had chores in childhood, but only a quarter ask their children to help with household duties today.[6] Some research indicates that one of the strongest predictors of success in life is whether children were given chores starting at three or four years old.[7] The daily average time spent in chores today is apparently 39.6 minutes for boys fifteen to nineteen years old, and 1.03 hours for girls.[8] I find those numbers difficult to believe.

My husband and I estimate that our six- and nine-year-olds spent an average of ten minutes per day doing chores before I started writing this book. I thought we had set a high bar, but the national average stunned me and compelled me to increase my expectations. Below, I've compiled a list of basic skills that our children would do well to master by eighteen.

1. Food: meal planning, grocery shopping, meal prep, clean up
2. Clothes: shopping, laundry, ironing, sewing
3. Home: cleaning, organizing, disposal, donation

4. Yard: pick up, mow, rake, water, garden
5. Money: earning, saving, giving, bank account, loans, investment, credit card
6. Relationships: assertiveness, apologies, boundaries, friendship, romance, healthy endings
7. Volunteer: free gift of time, money, resources
8. Vehicles: insurance, gas, cleaning, oil change, tire pressure, jump start
9. Faith: church, Bible, prayer
10. Time: alarm clock, schedule management

Of course, while learning to perform all these tasks, our children will bumble, annoy us, and want to give up. It is easier to do these things for them without their interference. We get it done better, faster, and with less grumbling. But if we do not pull our children in for hands-on training some of the time, how will they acquire these necessary skills? On average, fathers spend 20.4 minutes and mothers spend 31.2 minutes per day mentoring their children.[9] How much time do you spend per day or per week mentoring yours on these life skills? I know my time is usually lower than the average, especially for my older kiddos.

It smooths the process to decide in advance when we have the time, patience, and energy to tolerate a training session. Including a novice child in a tough task when we are harried or hurried doesn't tend to work well, often resulting in impatience and irritation.

Remember that blunders are part of the learning process, and each one deepens the training session—for all of us—if we look at it as life training. Our children are not supposed to be good at tasks they have not yet mastered. As the trainer, it is my responsibility to protect the session from my own agitation and engage in creative problem solving. So I admit to God when I'm losing my cool and ask for creative solutions and supernatural patience.

An angry, critical, intense trainer does more harm than good to the trainees. This time is for bonding with your children, helping them to accept their ignorance and imperfections, improving their skills, and building tolerance. This is a long-term endeavor. We must be willing to accept their inevitable mistakes while remaining gentle. We are building our children into men and women of character, and it is a long-term process.

Since I was inspired by writing this chapter, I have executed several new training sessions with my kids. I recently planned a grocery store training session for Henry. When Junie and Walter heard about it, they asked to join us.

Henry made the grocery list, read the aisle signs to find the food, scanned the items, paid with my card, and then helped haul the groceries inside. All three were invited to bring their own hard-earned money to buy themselves a treat. I let them know I would not be loaning or giving them any money. They could spend what they had. Walter only had enough to buy a small candy bar. Henry was able to purchase a toy car and candy. Junie decided that she wanted to save her money! Overall, it was a fun, rewarding experience as I went in thinking of everything I could ask of Henry to allow him ownership and responsibility for this task. The others were champing at the bit to copy their older brother. Henry said he enjoyed it and would like to do it again. We all experienced a sense of mastery and accomplishment—key components to building genuine self-esteem. Normally, I would have gone to the store alone for the sake of convenience and efficiency, and the kids would have stayed home—perhaps playing video games or watching cartoons. Let us make opportunities to show our children how even the mundane tasks of life can produce a sense of pride in offscreen accomplishment.

One of our most requested training sessions is car maintenance. Perhaps it runs in the blood, as my father and brother are mechanics. Our boys are obsessed with cars, NASCAR, and IndyCar. But even Junie has clamored to take part. We have taught them how to check and change the oil and how to put air in the tires. They were so proud of themselves for completing the tasks, and talked and bragged about it for days afterward. They replay the maintenance at home with their toys. No matter the task, there can be such joy in the completion. That's the kind of real-life satisfaction our children need to taste in increasing amounts to learn the thrill of offscreen accomplishment and the reward of a dirty job well done.

Our children want to feel important and skilled. They achieve some of that online and in video games as they progress to the next level. But having success in real life goes much further in developing a deep sense of efficacy, mastery, and self-esteem.

Our children need to be led, invited, coaxed, rewarded, and required to work. The earlier we start, the better the chance that they will cooperate and enjoy it. If your children are older and you have rarely or never brought them into intentional training sessions, consider the following approach.

"I was reading this book to learn how to be a better parent. I realize that I have not done much real-life training with you. I want to apologize to you for that. Take a look at this list with me. What do you wish you knew how to do better? Would you be willing to practice it with me? Let's set a time this weekend so that we can give it a shot."

If your child declines, wait a few days to revisit the topic. "You told me the other day that you weren't interested in any training. I understand your reluctance. I know you want to

_____ (insert activity of choice here) this weekend. I will be glad to take you after we've done a training session. You get to pick which chore we will tackle. So even though you don't care to do this, let me know what you pick, and I'll set it up for us."

Surly, seemingly lazy teens have confided in me that they wish their parents had taught them more real-world skills and allowed them to do more around the house. Learning progresses from ignorance to frustration, to failure, to improvement, to success, and finally to pride in one's work. If we do everything for our children, we are robbing them of this experience and setting them up for great struggles as adults. I wish children acquired a good work ethic and gratitude by observation alone, but they don't. In fact, the more privileges that are handed to them by hard-working parents, without effort on their part, the more entitled, bratty, expectant, and ungrateful they become.

Should we pay our children to do chores? Research suggests that unpaid chores benefit children more in the long run. We Bentons take a combination approach. We expect daily chores and random requests for help to be completed without pay. When my kids ask, "What will you give me for doing this?" I respond with the classic, "My undying respect and gratitude." We offer more difficult tasks with pay to whomever is willing to take them on, usually Junie. We keep a list of behaviors and tasks we are asking the kids to improve upon.

We intentionally add random tasks and requests frequently. The kids may grumble a bit about it. But as they become accustomed to our updated expectations, the complaining tends to decrease. We are trying to help them develop servants' hearts and a sense of shared responsibility for our home. Many of us parents believe it is our job to serve our children. I think that is true for the first two years of life. After that, it behooves our children to slowly but surely take responsibility for themselves, their possessions, and their lives. It is a rocky road, but it pays dividends.

Task mastery develops true self-esteem; excessive screen and social media use decrease it. Let's use real-life training and chores to build our children's confidence, sense of accomplishment, and healthy pride in themselves.

So prayerfully consider how you can implement these ideas with God's assistance so that your children will build responsible and interesting lives of satisfying accomplishment, both onscreen and offscreen.

CHAPTER 9

Recovering from Toxic Exposure and Screen Addiction

Despite your efforts to protect your child, what happens when you discover that he or she has been sucked into watching shocking, Pernicious content? You might feel powerless, helpless, angry, embarrassed, afraid, and sad in the face of this disturbing revelation. Dear parent, you are not alone, and you are not impotent. There is so much you can do to help turn this tide.

I suggest the following steps.

Before directly addressing your child, grieve and process the anger you feel with a safe peer and pray for guidance. "Lord, I am devastated to find out that my child has been watching pornography. I'm angry with him, with my spouse, with You, and with myself. Please guide me in handling this well so that I can save my child. In Jesus's name I pray."

Gently discover how, where, when, and why the child first interacted with the unhealthy content. You are likely angry with your child, but keep in mind that he was an innocent victim at the beginning. He was lured into a seductive temptation. He may have been more vulnerable to succumb because he has imperfect parents. The real enemy is not your child, who has probably been carrying fear and guilt over his secret actions and is now terrified of your response. Address it when you can speak with a calm, measured voice. "Kiddo, I found out you are watching pornography. It is probably startling and scary to hear this. I'll admit that I am angry, but mostly I'm worried about you. I need us to work together to be able to help you. First, I'm going to pray. Jesus, please join us in this conversation. Guide my words. Soften my child's heart to me so that we can speak openly about what has happened. Son, I need to ask you about this. We can talk now or in _____ (specify a time in the near future). We can talk with Daddy or just with me first. You choose." If your child refuses, firmly but kindly insist, and choose the option for him that you believe he would have preferred. "I'm sad that you are not making a choice, but I know you are overwhelmed, so I will choose for you. We will talk in an hour, just the two of us. Daddy will need to know about all of this, because he loves you too and we'll need his help. Do you want to ask or tell me anything else right now? Okay, then you can wait for me in your room and I will look for you in an hour. We'll be okay, and we will figure this out. I love you." Spend the time apart in prayer and talking with a safe peer for support and to temper your anger and fear.

Seek the child out at the appointed time. Bring a drink or a snack as a show of love that can help reduce the tension. "Okay, kiddo, time to talk. I'm going to pray again. Jesus, please comfort my child and help me to protect him better. Help him to speak openly and honestly with me. Son, I take responsibility that you have been drawn into watching porn. It is my job to protect you. I have obviously gone wrong somehow. I need to find out how I have failed you. I will be asking for your forgiveness when I fully understand my part in this. Please tell me about how you first saw porn and what happened after that." This approach will surprise your child and lower his defenses. And let's face it, if our children have been accessing Pernicious content without our knowledge, we are partially at fault. Continue with more gentle questions: "What do you think about porn? How do you feel before, during, and after you watch it? How and when do you access it? Who else has been involved with it?"

Validate what you can. Validating is not agreement or approval. It is expressing understanding. You might say, "I could see why this would interest you. It is popular, sexy, and seductive. I can understand your pursuit of this. In fact, I have seen porn myself, and it was very alluring." Tell more of your own experience at an age-appropriate level, sharing more headlines than details.

Reset the expectations and consequences. "How do you think this content aligns with our family values? What do you think God thinks about porn? Our family will not be engaging with this content because it isn't healthy for us. We need you to stop watching this material. We are concerned for you and know this content has affected you. We will have a session with a therapist to help us decide what support you might need." (This option should be considered depending how long your child has been engaging with the content, how upset he is by your discovery, and how contentious your relationship has been with him previously and as a result of this discovery. It never hurts to have a few consultations with a professional. It shows your child how important he is to you and how serious this matter is. And if his behavior has become a habit, it will be hard if not impossible to break without structured help. You can contact us at www.newlife.com for our network of counselors or join my online community and training program at www.dralicebenton.com.)

"Your behavior has broken our trust. This breaks our rules that we have previously discussed. You will lose access to your screens for a time. Because we have failed to protect you well enough, we will also make a sacrifice. We need to improve our parenting, and we want to support you. We have come up with several options for our own consequences, and we want you to choose what it will be (loss of social media, digital entertainment, alcohol, sweets, etc.). During the time you lose access to your screens, we will abstain alongside you.

"We will be giving you additional chores to do, which will be opportunities for you to rebuild trust with us as you cooperate and show a good and repentant attitude. You will be allowed to use your screens in public spaces in our home with one of us present for necessary schoolwork. We will be helping you fill the time you used to spend watching porn. We want you to identify a few activities you would be willing to do with us, like playing catch, a video game, or a bike ride.

"We will install a blocking and tracking system to help hold you and our whole family accountable. We will revisit this every week to decide how long these consequences will remain in place. The way you handle this will decide how quickly we can trust you and allow you more freedom and privilege.

"Let's pray again. Lord, we have all fallen short here. We need Your help to rebuild the safety in our home and to reestablish trust. Please help us all to be able to forgive one another and to choose Your way. Please help us all to overcome these temptations. We cannot do this without You. In Jesus's name we pray. Amen."

If your child refuses to answer any questions, consider saying, "I notice that you aren't willing to answer or speak. That is sad and frustrating. But I might feel the same way if I were in your shoes. It isn't appropriate not to answer, so I'll have to think of another consequence to add if you continue to choose to remain mute. I hope you choose to speak." Follow through with an additional consequence. For example, "You will be welcome to spend time with your friends after you talk this issue over with me."

Now let's try to understand how your child became involved with the toxic content.

Addictive behavior often begins because a lonely, discontented child is lured into a temptation. The temptation fills an internal emotional void. It meets a legitimate need in an illegitimate way. It relieves his loneliness, anxiety, depression, or feelings of inadequacy for a brief period. The child feels better. If the child's home environment is frequently stressful, he is much more likely to continue to turn to the unhealthy behavior in order to feel better again.

The child's imperfect parents have created a less-than-ideal home environment. You have fallen short in your parenting, as have we all. Addiction is a family disease, especially for a child. We parents have a high degree of responsibility for our child's vulnerability. The sooner we can accept that our character defects and unrepentant, unhealthy behavior laid a shaky foundation for our children, the better for all involved. We cannot force our child to change. But we can get the help we need to change, which will positively impact our children and give them the best chance of improving and breaking free of the addiction.

On a neurochemical level, the addictive behavior releases an enormous burst of the neurotransmitter dopamine, which is part of the reward circuit in the brain. The sensation of pleasure from the release of dopamine is part of our natural design that motivates us to repeat actions such as eating, exercising, and sex. This is a healthy, normal process that leads to learning and developing helpful behavior. Normally, once satiety has been reached, a negative feedback loop in the body signals us to disengage from the pleasurable activity.[1] The sensation of being full helps us to stop eating even though more delicious food is still available. The ability to cease a pleasurable activity is hampered by the child's overwhelming negative feelings, which he is attempting to soothe with pornography. As he begins to regularly turn to pornography for comfort, distraction, and excitement, he develops a habit. The behavior releases an abnormally large amount of dopamine and turns into a cycle of craving, obsession, and compulsion. This can result in addiction.

As the brain adjusts to the new, higher levels of dopamine, dependence and tolerance escalate. The child may begin to only feel pleasure when viewing porn. The enjoyment previously experienced in other activities pales in comparison to the rush porn provides, so the draw to pursue it strengthens. The child may feel increased depression when not using pornography. Over time, it may become the sole activity that produces a noticeable feeling of pleasure.

After a period of frequent use, the body develops a tolerance to the level of interest and excitement pornography elicits, and the viewer needs more porn or a different kind of content to achieve the same rush of dopamine and resulting pleasure, such as violence, multiple partners, same-sex interactions, or underage pornography. This progression is thought to be related to desensitization and appetite satiation in combination with the brain's reward system.[2] It is also the inescapable nature of unopposed sin. We are all vulnerable to it.

The child is driven to seek out pornography despite negative consequences such as parental disapproval, a guilty conscience, physical discomfort, lack of sleep, and incomplete academic or employment obligations. Ongoing usage eventually results in the loss of one's ability to limit the compulsive interaction with pornography. Any remaining self-control is overcome by the power of the addictive behavior.

I have worked in residential treatment facilities for substance use and have seen the lengths to which addicts go in their obsessive pursuit of the next high. Although using the substance was usually an act of free will at first, over time, the addict loses most, if not all, of his ability to choose differently. This statement may strike you as an absolution of the addict's personal responsibility, as if it isn't his fault that he chooses bad behavior. It is the ongoing choice and fault of a person to engage in unhealthy behavior. However, the longer the pattern continues, the more one's self-control atrophies. Please consider that we all engage in some behavior over which we have little to no control. We overeat, can't get ourselves to exercise, are too critical of ourselves and others, drink too much too often, procrastinate too much, have too much debt, etc. We all have behavior or attitudes that we have permitted to somewhat supersede our control. Despite the loss of control and diminished willpower over time, we still have the capacity to realize and admit our inability to change on our own and ask for help. And even that can feel insurmountable. So please allow grace for yourself and your family.

We could replace this example of pornography addiction with smartphone, gaming, or social media addiction. All these platforms have been scientifically fine-tuned to take advantage of our inbuilt dopaminergic pathways—and we know this because several high-ranking insiders, such as Chamath Palihapitiya (Facebook) and Tristan Harris (Google), have come forward to disclose this information as a warning and a plea.[3] They have explained that social media intentionally manipulates a reward schedule in order to exacerbate dependence and excessive checking. Likes on Facebook and streaks on Snapchat aren't just fun, they are intentionally programmed to be addictive. It is neither accidental nor coincidental; it is purposeful. Harris, who was previously employed as a design ethicist at Google, explains that "brain hacking" is one element of a more extensive playbook used to construct social media, like a Las Vegas slot machine that keeps you coming back for more. Programmers have realized that a continuous scroll without end will keep us looking longer. Some social media platforms intentionally withhold reactions to photos and posts. During that period of "silence," we experience an increase of cortisol and anxiety that is relieved only by checking our phones again and again. The accumulated likes are then released in a burst that generates an increase of dopamine and a resolution of the anxiety.[4]

Most social media is free to us consumers. We don't pay money to use the systems, but we do pay in an even more valuable asset: our time, attention, personal information, and personal data. Programmers are paid to get us checking as obsessively and addictively as possible. And most of us and our children are playing right into the trap, unaware of how habitual and subconscious our constant checking has become. Most of us check our phones every fifteen minutes or less, regardless of any alerts they may give us.[5]

The American Psychological Association, in its most recent Diagnostic and Statistical Manual, recognizes Internet Gaming Disorder as a dysfunctional pattern of behavior.[6] It is not yet an official diagnosis. Researchers are identifying similar patterns of digital activity, including Internet

Addiction, Smartphone Addiction, Social Media Addiction, and Problematic Smartphone Use (PSU) as concerning behavior that shares characteristics of substance addiction.

Some of the related symptoms include engaging in digital activity at a level and frequency that impairs daily functioning, missing work, and having difficulty concentrating on work, school, or relationships due to digital use. Those with problematic digital use may experience physical pain in their wrists and necks. They may not be able to tolerate lack of digital access. They may feel distressed if they are separated from their phones or screens. They may check for updates and digital communication constantly with a fear of missing out. (See the FOMO questionnaire in chapter 2.) They may continue their level of digital activity despite negative consequences. Others may notice and express concern over it. Tolerance can be developed in which a previous level of digital use is no longer satisfying, and the use escalates. There is also withdrawal when the person is separated from digital use, including physical discomfort, anxiety, agitation, and depressive symptoms. Those who smoke and drink alcohol are more likely to develop PSU, as are those who experience anxiety, depression, low self-esteem, and low self-control.[7]

I have slightly adjusted the wording of a ten-question scale developed to assess Problematic Smartphone Use (PSU)[8] to enhance its readability. Circle the number that best fits your level of disagreement or agreement with the listed behavior. Add up your responses for your total score. A score of 31 or higher for males suggests PSU, and a score of 33 or more suggests PSU for females. The cutoff score is differentiated because in research, females have fairly consistently displayed more self-awareness and self-report of their PSU.

We have a void within us—an unquenchable thirst that can only be truly satisfied by relationships with our Creator and safe, stable, warm people. If the void remains empty, we will attempt to fill it with something else: screen distraction, gaming, food, alcohol, drugs, sex, violence, money, or status. Any of these superficial substitutes can result in eventual abusive or addictive behavior that will lead to some level of decay or death in our lives and relationships.

The solution to break free is always increasing our investment in relationship with God and trustworthy companions. Dr. Bob Smith and Bill Wilson formatted the Twelve Steps as a structured process to rebuild relationship, repent of the unhealthy behavior pattern, and regain self-control.[9] In my opinion, all families would benefit from working the steps together. If you and your children do not need these principles now, you will need them eventually. Because let's face facts, folks, even if we avoid developing an addiction to

Problematic Smartphone Use (PSU)		Strongly Disagree	Disagree	Somewhat Disagree	Somewhat Agree	Agree	Strongly Agree
1	I miss planned work due to my smartphone use.	1	2	3	4	5	6
2	I have a hard time concentrating in class, while doing assignments, or while working due to smartphone use.	1	2	3	4	5	6
3	I feel pain in my wrists or at the back of my neck while using a smartphone.	1	2	3	4	5	6
4	I wouldn't be able to stand not having my smartphone.	1	2	3	4	5	6
5	I feel impatient and fretful when I am not holding my smartphone.	1	2	3	4	5	6
6	My smartphone is on my mind even when I am not using it.	1	2	3	4	5	6
7	I will never give up using my smartphone even when my daily life is already greatly affected by it.	1	2	3	4	5	6
8	I constantly check my smartphone so as not to miss conversations between other people on social media.	1	2	3	4	5	6
9	I use my smartphone longer than I intend to use it.	1	2	3	4	5	6
10	The people around me tell me that I use my smartphone too much.	1	2	3	4	5	6
	Total						

pornography, substances, or screens, we all have a sin addiction problem. And none of us maintains sobriety from sins for very long. Intentionally or unintentionally, we all harm each other at some point. The principles that undergird the Twelve Steps help us to get back on track and stay on track.

Opinions vary on the effectiveness of recovery from addictive behavior. It is well known that the relapse rate for any addiction is high, and available treatments are woefully inadequate. Nonetheless, those who fully participate in the tenets of recovery show longer abstinence from their addiction than those who do not engage in an Alcoholics Anonymous-style recovery program.[10]

Twelve-Step Recovery as Applied to Problematic Screen Use[11]

1. I admit that I am powerless over my unhealthy behavior, including screen use, which has become unmanageable or difficult to control.
2. I believe in a power greater than myself, God, who can restore my self-control.
3. I decide to turn my will and my life over to God through Jesus Christ.

4. I have made a searching and fearless moral inventory of myself, especially as it relates to my screen use.

5. I admit to God, myself, and another human being the nature of my unhealthy screen use.

6. I am ready to have God remove my defects of character.

7. I humbly ask God to remove my shortcomings.

8. I have made a list of all the people I have harmed online and offline, and I am willing to make amends to them.

9. I have made direct amends to such people wherever possible, except when to do so would injure them or others.

10. I continue to take personal inventory of my screen use, and when I am wrong, I admit it.

11. I have sought, through prayer and meditation, to improve my conscious contact with God, praying for knowledge of His will for me, and the power to carry that out.

12. Having a spiritual awakening as the result of these steps, I try to carry this message to others with Problematic Screen Use and to practice these principles in all my affairs.

Let's break this down into nine potential dinner conversations.

Dinner 1: Ideally, the father (but whichever parent is willing) says, "Folks, I want to confess to you that my _____ (type of screen use) is somewhat out of control. I keep trying to decrease my use of _____ (type of screen use), but I find myself checking my phone multiple times per day. I want to confess to you all that I'm failing to rein it in. In fact, I admit that on my own, I'm powerless to change this problem, because I have been trying for years and have made limited progress. Is there anything that feels out of control in your thoughts, emotions, or behavior? Could we do a family confession?"

Do not force participation. Modeling is more effective than coercion.

Dinner 2: Parent says, "I want God's help to change my phone use. I cannot do this without Him. I believe He can give me the power I lack on my own. Do any of you want God's help to change something about yourselves? Let's ask for it together in prayer."

Dinner 3: Parent says, "I'm going to recommit my life to God. I realize I have not fully surrendered my screen use to Him. I want to surrender that now in front of all of you. Would you pray for me? Lord, I invite You into all areas of my life. I am too attached to my phone. I desperately need

Your help. I'm powerless to change on my own. I surrender to You."

Dinner 4: Parent says, "I've been thinking about my phone use, and I realize I have done some damage. I want to confess it to you all. I've been distracted, and I know it frustrates you when you are trying to talk with me. I work too hard and too long, and you all miss me. Sometimes I'm looking at garbage on my phone, like Hollywood gossip, and it is a poor use of my time. I've been critical of all of you and tried to impose rules on you when I'm not even doing well with my own phone."

Dinner 5: Parent says, "Tonight, in your presence, I officially ask God to remove my defects of character, particularly my unhealthy phone use."

Dinner 6: Parent says, "I need to make amends to all of you for prioritizing my screens and my work above you. I apologize and ask for your forgiveness. I want you each to think of an activity that you would like to do with me without my screen in hand. I want to spend some time one on one with each of you to make up for some of the hurt that I've caused. Would you please forgive me?"

Do not demand forgiveness. Accept their "no" or "not yet."

Dinner 7: Parent says, "I've been trying to be better with my screens, but I realized I was on social media again for too long when you were asking for homework help. Did I use my screens in any other way recently that frustrated you?"

Dinner 8: Parent says, "I want to pray with you all as my witnesses tonight. God, I want to spend regular time with You, but I'm inconsistent. I ask for Your help to do so. I want to know Your will for my life and live it out."

Dinner 9: Parent says, "I'm still imperfectly trying to keep a healthy balance of onscreen and offscreen time. I want to help you folks with anything you are struggling with, too. Is there anything with which you would like my help?"

If you as a parent have done little of your own recovery work for your character defects, you should first go through the twelve steps privately with a peer or small group rather than with your family. You need to clean up your side of the street so that you can subsequently lead your family by your modeling. If your home has been filled with chronic or frequent parental anger, criticism, coldness, or authoritarian discipline, I recommend meeting with a therapist first. This applies whether you have been the perpetrating parent or a victim of your spouse's unhealthy anger. New Life maintains a network of counselors across the country who can help you (www.newlife.com.) You can also access my online parenting community and parent-training program dedicated to the application of this material through www.dralicebenton.com.

To summarize: children who are feeling anxious, depressed, and lonely, living in homes with high levels of parental criticism, anger, conflict, arguments, neglect, or enabling, are at higher risk of developing an addictive behavior and/or problematic screen use. Parents who engage in addictive behavior increase the likelihood that their children will follow suit.

We have a true spiritual enemy who is actively working to lure all of us into unhealthy, sinful, addictive behavior. He will tempt parents and children alike to choose superficial means of soothing discomfort and eliciting excitement. The major social media outlets and gaming programmers are employing the principles of addiction to keep us all checking and using their systems.

We can combat this by becoming Mentor parents who purposefully bring our children online with us to show them the joys, blessing, relationship engagement, and convenience screens can offer. We can teach them that distress is best relieved in safe relationships through regularly offering the Comfort Circle. We can increase self-control by accessing the supernatural power God offers us through the Bible. We can raise our expectations for ourselves and our children to those God has set for us, in part through the Ten Commandments. We can use screens as a leveraging tool to increase our children's motivation and to improve their appreciation for the privileges we provide for them. We can safeguard our homes, eyes, and ears and thus protect our children's hearts, minds, and souls. We can seek greater parental alignment by cleaning up our side of the street and gently, kindly, and humbly inviting our spouse to join us without trying to control him or her. We can face the true enemy head on, equipped with the mighty name of Jesus and spiritual armor. We can increase our children's self-esteem, confidence, and sense of accomplishment by engaging them in real-life training to find their God-given purpose. And we can model for our children that we are all broken and in need of healing by addressing our own and our family's unhealthy and addictive behaviors through the twelve steps of recovery.

Folks, if this book has helped you, please consider passing your copy on to another family or buying a new one for them. I believe that all families could benefit from this content. Share your story with us about how this book has impacted you.

You do not need to try to practice all of this on your own. Please contact us at either www.newlife.com or www.dralice-benton.com so that we can accompany you in this process.

Frequently Asked Questions

At what age should I allow my child to have a cell phone?

I recommend allowing a respectful, responsible, trustworthy, hard-working child over the age of three to be allowed to use a *family* cell phone that does not have access to the internet, such as a Pinwheel or Gabb Phone, on a limited basis. I would be hard pressed to give my children under sixteen their own phone with full internet access. This restriction allows ongoing protection and use of the leveraging principles. Children can use parents' phones or the family computer for internet access under supervision. I would consider, on a case-by-case basis, giving a child between the ages of sixteen and eighteen a phone with internet access so that they are prepared for the freedom they will have as adults. I would consider making an exception for a teen of superb character proven over years of consistency, but I would expect him or her to help foot the monthly bill. It would still be a parent-owned phone, and their access would still depend on their behavior and attitude.

How much digital entertainment per day should I allow?

The American Academy of Pediatrics recommends that digital entertainment should be avoided for children under eighteen months and suggests that only Enriching content should be slowly introduced from eighteen to twenty-four months. Children from two to five years old are encouraged to enjoy up to one hour per day of enriching content, ideally coviewing with parents who are actively engaged.[1] Does that sound like a shockingly small amount? It is in comparison to the normal amount of digital consumption for most children.

If we are following the principles laid out in this book—building a relational, spiritual, disciplined, purposeful, and fulfilling life with our children—then their downtime available for digital entertainment should naturally be fairly limited. So in applying the leverage principle, our children are welcome to digital entertainment after they have completed their homework and chores. In our family, we generally keep our digital entertainment to two hours or fewer on school days and two to four hours on weekends. This is a guideline for us rather than a hard-and-fast rule. Unless we are watching a movie or a sporting event, my husband and I try to break the digital entertainment time up into twenty-minute intervals, sometimes requiring our children to set a timer for themselves. When the time is up, we might ask them to play outside, tidy a mess, entertain themselves offscreen, or play a board game with us, after which they might be welcome to more time. It certainly takes effort and monitoring, but to us, the benefits are worth the cost.

My husband and I want our family life to be so full, interesting, fun, and challenging offscreen that our time onscreen is supplementary rather than primary. This is an ongoing work in progress to strive for and a tension to be managed.

Which internet filter software programs do you recommend?

I recommend Bark and Qustodio for filtering and alerting parents.

Do you recommend GPS monitoring of my child's location?

I find GPS tracking to be helpful in emergency situations. I see a risk for anxious or controlling parents to obsessively check and follow their children's movements. Relying regularly on GPS tracking can unintentionally replace the necessary trust-building that should be expected from an adolescent and teen. Consider whether it would be a blessing or a burden to you and your child to have constant knowledge of his or her location.

Which types of treatment do you recommend for screen-related addiction?

We recommend the New Life Recovery groups, which can be accessed at www.newlife.com, Alice's online parent training programs (www.dralicebenton.com), and the Twelve-Step program provided by Internet and Technology Addicts Anonymous (www.internetaddictsanonymous.org).

At what time of night should we shut down screens?

Quality of sleep significantly impacts overall well-being. Evening use of portable screens, especially in bed, leads to less sleep and poorer quality.[2] Chronically disturbed sleep increases vulnerability to anxiety, depression, suicidal thoughts, and even psychotic symptoms (after days with no sleep whatsoever)! So, I recommend docking screens outside of children's bedrooms at night. It helps if parents are also willing to model putting their phones away or shutting them down for the night.

The blue light used in screens suppresses the release of melatonin and causes a person to be more awake and alert. The body's circadian rhythm is designed to respond to the light of the sun during the day and darkness at night. Too much light during the evening hours sends the brain the message that it is still time to remain awake and alert. It can shift a person's circadian rhythm off-kilter by one to three hours![3] In other words, if your child normally fell asleep at 9 p.m., prolonged, late-night exposure to blue light could shift his sleep period to midnight. So turning screens off at least an hour before bedtime allows the brain to receive the signal that darkness means sleep.

Does excessive screen use damage eyes?

The American Optometric Association (AOA) reports that prolonged digital reading can lead to Digital Eyestrain Syndrome, with symptoms that include headaches, blurred vision, dry eyes, and neck and shoulder pain. The AOA recommends the 20:20:20 technique, which involves taking a twenty-second break and focusing the eyes about twenty feet away for every twenty minutes of digital reading.[4]

What if my spouse is addicted to Pernicious content?

Please know that you are not alone in this situation. You may know that New Life's primary mission is to help men struggling with pornography. Consider asking your spouse to read this book, as well as *Every Man's Battle*. New Life also offers the Every Man's Battle Workshop every month. The Restore Workshop is for the spouses of men struggling with sexual integrity. Al-Anon is the twelve-step recovery program that supports and guides the spouses of addicts. Groups can be found at https://al-anon.org/.

Acknowledgments

From Alice Benton:

Lord, thank You for giving me the opportunity to coauthor this book with Steve. You continuously inspired and energized me during the writing process. May it bring glory to Your holy name and inspire families to love better and to use screens in a way that honors You and blesses their children.

Steve, you are my mentor. My life is immensely better because of all that I have learned from you. Thank you for taking the risk of allowing me to audition for the radio show and to coauthor with you.

Dear Hoosb, The Henz, Nunie, Walt, and Vincent Marchuski—goodness gracious, you folks have put up with Mamma working a whole lot. Thank you for all of your prayers, cheerleading, and for being quiet while Mamma works for just another fifteen minutes. Thank you for letting me experiment with all these ideas on you. I am so blessed to keep waking up to another day with you. Please keep putting up with me. I'll get better at this, I promise.

Pappa and Mom, you did a darn good job raising us rascals. Thank you for sacrificing your hours, days, and years to us four kids. I love you.

To all of you who have allowed me the privilege of serving you, thank you. You have helped me to test and refine these ideas.

To my gals' group, you know all my ugliest sins and temptations, and you love me anyhow. You are my life group. Thank you for Saturday mornings.

To the New Life Crew, I am honored to be a part of the ministry with you. You have taught me so much. Thank you for having me.

From Stephen Arterburn:

Our editor at Salem Books, Karla Dial, accepted the challenge of working with someone who had never written a book and someone who had written too many. What you read is a result of her hard work and commitment to "getting it right." Thank you, Karla, for all you have done to make the best of what we have provided you.

A huge thank-you to Tim Peterson, who believed in this project and made it happen. You are one of the best in the publishing world, and I am grateful for every project we do together.

Finally, Greg Johnson, thank you for all you have done to help me find new ways to create projects that address unmet needs. You are a great man, and it is a great joy to work with you.

Notes

Chapter One: Are Your Children Getting Enough Screen Time with You?

1. Sei Yon Sohn et al., "Prevalence of Problematic Smartphone Usage and Associated Mental Health Outcomes amongst Children and Young People: A Systematic Review, Meta-Analysis and GRADE of the Evidence," *BMC Psychiatry* 19, no. 356 (2019), https://doi.org/10.1186/s12888-019-2350-x.

2. José De Sola et al., "Prevalence of Problematic Cell Phone Use in an Adult Population in Spain as Assessed by the Mobile Phone Problem Use Scale," *PLoS ONE* 12, no. 8 (2017), https://doi.org/10.1371/journal.pone.0181184; Laurel Felt and Michael Robbb, *Technology Addiction: Concern, Controversy, and Finding Balance* (San Francisco: Common Sense Media, 2016), https://www.commonsensemedia.org/sites/default/files/research

/report/csm_2016_technology_addiction_research_brief_0.pdf; Min Kwon et al., "The Smartphone Addiction Scale: Development and Validation of a Short Version for Adolescents," *PLoS ONE* 8, no. 12 (2013), https://doi.org/10.1371/journal.pone.0083558.

3. Alexandra Samuel, "Parents: Reject Technology Shame," *The Atlantic*, November 4, 2015, https://www.theatlantic.com /technology/archive/2015/11/why-parents-shouldnt-feel -technology-shame/414163.

4. Paige Mayer, "Research Confirms the Ideal Digital Parenting Style," OurPact, November 25, 2016, https://medium.com/@ ourpactapp/research-confirms-the-ideal-digital-parenting-style -7f13ce0b6769.

5. Sally Maeng and Kelly Arbeau, "#TheStruggleIsReal: Fear of Missing Out (FOMO) and Nomophobia Can, but Do Not Always, Occur Together," ResearchGate, September 2018, https://www.researchgate.net/publication/327477166 _TheStruggleIsReal_Fear_of_missing_out_FoMO_and _nomophobia_can_but_do_not_always_occur_together.

6. Alexandra Samuel,"Six Ways to Be a Digital Mentor to Your Kid," JSTOR Daily, August 22, 2017, https://daily.jstor.org /6-ways-digital-mentor-kids.

Chapter Two: Comfort

1. Jenny Radesky et al., "Patterns of Mobile Device Use by Caregivers and Children during Meals in Fast Food Restaurants," *Pediatrics* 133, no. 4 (2014): 843–9, https://doi.org/10.1542/ peds.2013-3703.

2. Victoria Rideout and Michael Robb, *The Common Sense Census: Media Use by Kids Age Zero to Eight* (San Francisco: Common Sense Media, 2017), https://www.common sensemedia.org/sites/default/files/research/report/csm_zeroto eight_fullreport_release_2.pdf.

3. Radesky, "Patterns of Mobile Device Use"; Brandon McDaniel and Jenny Radesky, "Technoference: Longitudinal Associations between Parent Technology Use, Parenting Stress, and Child Behavior Problems," *Pediatric Research* 84 (June 2018): 210–18, https://doi.org/10.1038/s41390-018-0052-6.

4. Marjut Wallenius, Raija-Leena Punamäki, and Arja Rimpela, "Digital Game Playing and Direct and Indirect Aggression in Early Adolescence: The Roles of Age, Social Intelligence, and Parent-Child Communication," *Journal of Youth and Adolescence* 36, no. 3 (2007): 325–36, https://doi.org/10.1007/s10964-006-9151-5.

5. Tamara Afifi et al., "WIRED: The Impact of Media and Technology Use on Stress (Cortisol) and Inflammation (Interleukin IL-6) in Fast Paced Families," *Computers in Human Behavior* 81 (2018): 265–73, https://doi.org/10.1016/j.chb.2017.12.010.

6. Holly Rus and Jitske Tiemensma, "Social Media under the Skin: Facebook Use after Acute Stress Impairs Cortisol Recovery," *Frontiers in Psychology* 8 (2017), https://doi.org/10.3389/fpsyg.2017.01609.

7. E. Bun Lee, "Facebook Use and Texting among African American and Hispanic Teenagers: An Implication for Academic Performance," *Journal of Black Studies* 45, no. 2 (2014): 83–101, https://doi.org/10.1177/0021934713519819.

8. Roy Pea et al., "Media Use, Face-to-Face Communication, Media Multitasking, and Social Well-Being among 8- to 12-Year-Old Girls," *Developmental Psychology* 48, no. 2 (2012): 327–36, https://doi.org/10.1037/a0027030.

9. Larry Rosen et al., "Is Facebook Creating 'iDisorders'? The Link between Clinical Symptoms of Psychiatric Disorders and Technology Use, Attitudes and Anxiety," *Computers in Human Behavior* 29, no. 3 (May 2013): 1243–54, https://doi.org/10.1016/j.chb.2012.11.012.

10. Sally Maeng and Kelly Arbeau, "#TheStruggleIsReal: Fear of Missing Out (FOMO) and Nomophobia Can, but Do Not Always, Occur Together," ResearchGate, September 2018, https://www.researchgate.net/publication/327477166 _TheStruggleIsReal_Fear_of_missing_out_FoMO_and _nomophobia_can_but_do_not_always_occur_together.

11. Benjamin Riordan et al., "The Development of a Single Item FOMO (Fear of Missing Out) Scale," *Current Psychology* 39 (2020): 1215–20, https://doi.org/10.1007/s12144-018-9824-8.

12. Andrew Przybylski et al., "Motivational, Emotional, and Behavioral Correlates of Fear of Missing Out," *Computers in Human Behavior* 29, no. 4 (2013): 1841–48, https://doi.org/10.1016/j.chb.2013.02.014.

13. Ali Zeinali et al., "The Mediational Pathway among Parenting Styles, Attachment Styles and Self-Regulation with Addiction Susceptibility of Adolescents," *Journal of Research in Medical Sciences* 16, no. 9 (2011): 1105–21, https://www.ncbi.nlm.nih.gov/pmc/articles/PMC3430035.

14. Denise Rizzolo et al., "Stress Management Strategies for Students: The Immediate Effects of Yoga, Humor, and Reading on Stress," *Journal of College Teaching and Learning* 6, no. 8 (2009): 79–88, https://doi.org/10.19030/tlc.v6i8.1117.

15. Raymond Mar, Keith Oatley, and Jordan Peterson, "Exploring the Link between Reading Fiction and Empathy: Ruling Out Individual Differences and Examining Outcomes," *Communications* 34, no. 4 (2009): 34, 407–28, https://doi.org/10.1515/COMM.2009.025.

16. Gary Cooney et al., "Exercise for Depression," *Cochrane Database of Systematic Reviews* 2013, no. 9 (2013), https://doi.org/10.1002/14651858.CD004366.pub6; Chanudda Nabkasorn et al., "Effects of Physical Exercise on Depression, Neuroendocrine Stress Hormones and Physiological Fitness in Adolescent Females with Depressive Symptoms," *European Journal of Public Health* 16, no. 2 (2006): 179–84, https://doi.org/10.1093/eurpub/cki159.

Chapter Three: Self-Control

1. Michael McCullough and Evan Carter, "Religion, Self-Control, and Self-Regulation: How and Why Are They Related?" *APA*

Handbook of Psychology, Religion, and Spirituality 1 (2015): 123–38, https://doi.org/10.1037/14045-006.

2. Ting Tao et al., "Development of Self-Control in Children Aged 3 to 9 Years: Perspective from a Dual-Systems Model," Scientific Reports 4 (2014): article 7272, https://doi.org/10.1038/srep07272.

3. Erik Erikson, Identity and the Life Cycle (New York: W. W. Norton Company, 1980).

4. Center for Bible Engagement, On the Verge of Walking Away? American Teens, Communication with God, and Temptations (Lincoln, Nebraska: Back to the Bible, 2009), https://bttbfiles.com/web/docs/cbe/On_the_Verge_of_Walking_Away.pdf.

5. Center for Bible Engagement, Reading Plans and Bible Engagement (Lincoln, Nebraska: Back to the Bible, 2009), https://bttbfiles.com/web/docs/cbe/Reading_Plans_and_Bible_Engagement.pdf.

6. Arnold Cole and Pamela Caudill Ovwigho, Understanding the Bible Engagement Challenge: Scientific Evidence for the Power of 4 (Lincoln, Nebraska: Back to the Bible, 2009), https://bttbfiles.com/web/docs/cbe/Scientific_Evidence_for_the_Power_of_4.pdf.

7. Ibid.

8. McCullough and Carter, "Religion, Self-Control, and Self-Regulation: How and Why Are They Related?"

9. Center for Bible Engagement, On the Verge of Walking Away?

10. Andrew Greeley, *Faithful Attraction* (New York: Tom Doherty Associates, 1991); Rebecca Marín, Andrew Christensen, and David Atkins, "Infidelity and Behavioral Couple Therapy: Relationship Outcomes over 5 Years Following Therapy," *Couple and Family Psychology: Research and Practice* 3, no. 1 (2014): 1–12, https://doi.org/10.1037/cfp0000012.

Chapter Four: Reset Your Expectations

1. Zeinali et al., "The Mediational Pathway among Parenting Styles, Attachment Styles and Self-Regulation with Addiction Susceptibility of Adolescents," *Journal of Research in Medical Sciences* 16, no. 9 (2011): 1105–21, https://www.ncbi.nlm.nih.gov/pmc/articles/PMC3430035.

2. Marjorie Gunnoe, E. Mavis Hetherington, and David Reiss, "Parental Religiosity, Parenting Style, and Adolescent Social Responsibility," *The Journal of Early Adolescence* 19, no. 2 (May 1999): 199–225, https://doi.org/10.1177/0272431699019002004.

3. Ali Zeinali et al., "The Mediational Pathway among Parenting Styles, Attachment Styles and Self-Regulation with Addiction Susceptibility of Adolescents."

4. Ibid.

5. Gunnoe, Hetherington, and Reiss, "Parental Religiosity, Parenting Style, and Adolescent Social Responsibility"; M. McCullough and Evan Carter, "Religion, Self-Control, and Self-Regulation: How and Why Are They Related?" *APA Handbook of Psychology, Religion, and Spirituality* 1 (2015): 123–38, https://doi.org/10.1037/14045-006.

6. Ibid.
7. John Coffman, *Coffman Commentaries on the Bible* (Abilene, Kansas: Abilene Christian University Press, 1983).
8. Center for Bible Engagement, *On the Verge of Walking Away? American Teens, Communication with God, and Temptations* (Lincoln, Nebraska: Back to the Bible, 2009), https://bttbfiles .com/web/docs/cbe/On_the_Verge_of_Walking_Away.pdf.
9. Coffman, *Coffman Commentaries on the Bible*.
10. Jean Twenge et al., "Age, Period, and Cohort Trends in Mood Disorder Indicators and Suicide Related Outcomes in a Nationally Representative Dataset," *Journal of Abnormal Psychology* 128, no. 3 (2019): 185–199, https://doi.org/10.1037 /abn0000410.
11. "TelAbortion," Gynuity Health Projects, https://mgaleg .maryland.gov/cmte_testimony/2021/hgo/1dZSelJ3tXUIXwW _ICEGETJijUR3n0qcg.pdf.
12. Gynuity Health Projects (@Gynuity), "We acknowledge the multitude of barriers youth face…," Twitter, August 12, 2020, 2:46 p.m., https://twitter.com/Gynuity/status/129361744 8260968448.
13. U.S. Food and Drug Administration, "Questions and Answers on Mifeprex," https://www.fda.gov/drugs/postmarket-drug -safety-information-patients-and-providers/questions-and -answers-mifeprex.
14. Revealing Reality, *Young People, Pornography, and Age-Verification* (London: British Board of Film Classification, 2019), https://www.revealingreality.co.uk/wp-content/uploads

/2020/01/BBFC-Young-people-and-pornography-Final-report
-2401.pdf.

15. Sheri Madigan et al. , "Prevalence of Multiple Forms of Sexting
Behavior among Youth: A Systematic Review and Meta-Analysis,"
JAMA Pediatrics 172, no. 4 (2018): 327–35, https://doi.org/
10.1001/jamapediatrics.2017.5314.

16. United States Code, "Title 18, Citizen's Guide To U.S. Federal
Law on Obscenity," Office of the Law Revision Counsel,
updated November 9, 2021, https://www.justice.gov/criminal
-ceos/citizens-guide-us-federal-law-obscenity.

17. Zoe Kleinman, "My Son Spent £3,160 in One Game," BBC
News, July 15, 2019, www.bbc.com/news/technology
-48925623.

18. Doree Lewak, "This 6-Year-Old Racked up $16K on Mom's
Credit Card Playing Video Games," *New York Post*, December
12, 2020, https://nypost.com/2020/12/12/this-6-year-old
-racked-up-over-16k-on-his-moms-credit-card.

19. Coffman, *Coffman Commentaries on the Bible*.

20. Dennis Prager, *The Ten Commandments, Still the Best Moral
Code* (Washington, D.C.: Regnery Publishing, 2015).

21. Sally Maeng and Kelly Arbeau, "#TheStruggleIsReal: Fear of
Missing Out (FOMO) and Nomophobia Can, but Do Not
Always, Occur Together," ResearchGate, September 2018,
https://www.researchgate.net/publication/327477166
_TheStruggleIsReal_Fear_of_missing_out_FoMO_and
_nomophobia_can_but_do_not_always_occur_together.

Chapter Five: Access as Leverage

1. Victoria Rideout and Michael Robb, *The Common Sense Census: Media Use by Kids Age Zero to Eight* (San Francisco: Common Sense Media, 2020), https://www.commonsense media.org/sites/default/files/research/report/csm_zerotoeight_fullreport_release_2.pdf.
2. Foster Cline and Jim Fay, *Parenting with Love and Logic* (Carol Stream, Illinois: Nav Press, [1990] 2006).
3. "5 Major Moments in Cellphone History," Canadian Broadcasting Corporation, April 13, 2013, www.cbc.ca/amp /1.1407352.

Chapter Six: Focusing on What Is Pure

1. Natalie Coyle, "The Psychology of Horror Games," *Psychology and Video Games* (blog), November 19, 2020, http://platinum paragon.info/psychology-of-horror-games.
2. Joanne Cantor and Kristen Harrison, "Tales from the Screen: Enduring Fright Reactions to Scary Media," *Media Psychology* 1, no. 2 (1999): 97–116, https://doi.org/10.1207/s1532785x mep0102_1; See also Marc Andersen et al., "Playing with Fear: A Field Study in Recreational Horror," *Psychological Science* 31, no. 12, (2020): 1497–1510, https://doi.org/10.1177/0956 797620972116.
3. Cantor and Harrison, "Tales from the Screen: Enduring Fright Reactions to Scary Media."
4. Ibid.

5. Marvin Zuckerman, *Sensation Seeking and Risky Behavior* (Los Angeles: American Psychological Association, 2007), https://doi.org/10.1037/11555-000.

6. Ibid.

7. Coyle, "The Psychology of Horror Games."

8. Mayumi Okuda et al., "Do Parenting Behaviors Modify the Way Sensation Seeking Influences Antisocial Behaviors?" *Journal of Child Psychology and Psychiatry* 60, no. 2 (2019): 169–77, https://doi.org/10.1111/jcpp.12954.

Chapter Seven: Parental Disagreement

1. E. Mark Cummings et al., "Interparental Conflict in Kindergarten and Adolescent Adjustment: Prospective Investigation of Emotional Security as an Explanatory Mechanism," *Child Development* 83, no. 5 (2012): 1703–15, https://doi.org/10.1111/j.1467-8624. 2012.01807.x.

2. Ibid.

Chapter Eight: Building an Interesting Offscreen Life

1. Canadian Red Cross, "We Are the Lucky Ones," https:// www.redcross.ca/crc/documents/What-We-Do/Emergencies-and-Disasters-WRLD/education-resources/lucky_ones_ povdisease.pdf.

2. Victoria Rideout and Michael Robb, *Social Media, Social Life: Teens Reveal Their Experiences* (San Francisco: Common Sense Media, 2018), https://www.commonsensemedia.org/sites

/default/files/research/report/2018-social-media-social-life
-executive-summary-web.pdf.

3. Victoria Rideout et al., *Coping with COVID-19: How Young People Use Digital Media to Manage Their Mental Health* (San Francisco: Common Sense and Hopelab, 2021), https://www.chcf.org/publication/coping-covid-19-young-people-digital-media-manage-mental-health.

4. Victoria Rideout, *Zero to Eight: Children's Media Use in America* (San Francisco: Common Sense Media, 2011), https://www.ftc.gov/sites/default/files/documents/public_comments/california-00325%C2%A0/00325-82243.pdf.

5. Rideout et al., *Coping with COVID-19*.

6. Ami Albernaz, "Sparing Chores Spoils Children and Their Future Selves, Study Says," *The Boston Globe*, December 8, 2015, https://www.bostonglobe.com/lifestyle/2015/12/08/research-indicates-sparing-chores-spoils-children-and-their-future-selves/ZLvMznpC5btmHtNRXXhNFJ/story.html.

7. Marty Rossmann, "Getting Children Involved in Household Tasks: Is it Worth the Effort?," *Family Forum* (Saint Paul, Minnesota: Minnesota Council on Family Relations, Winter 2003): 5, https://mn.ncfr.org/wp-content/uploads/sites/3/2014/02/2003_winter.pdf.

8. Bureau of Labor Statistics, "Table 11A. Time Spent in Leisure and Sports Activities for the Civilian Population by Selected Characteristics, Averages per Day, 2019 Annual Averages," *American Time Use Survey*, U. S. Department of Labor, last

updated June 25, 2020, https://www.bls.gov/news.release/atus
.t11A.htm.

9. Ibid.

Chapter Nine: Recovering from Toxic Exposure and Addiction

1. Julia Christensen, "Pleasure Junkies All Around! Why It
   Matters and Why 'the Arts' Might Be the Answer: A
   Biopsychological Perspective," *Proceedings of the Royal Society
   B: Biological Sciences* 284, no. 1854 (May 17, 2017), https://
   doi.org/10.1098/rspb.2016.2837.

2. Kathryn Seigfried-Spellar and Marcus Rogers, "Does Deviant
   Porn Use Follow a Guttman-like Progression?," *Computers in
   Human Behavior* 29, no. 5 (September 2013): 1997–2003,
   https://doi.org/10.1016/j.chb.2013.04.018.

3. Trevor Haynes, "Dopamine, Smartphones, and You: A Battle
   for Your Time," *Harvard University Graduate School of Arts
   and Sciences* (blog), *Harvard University*, May 1, 2018,
   https://sitn.hms.harvard.edu/flash/2018/dopamine-smartphones-
   battle-time; Anderson Cooper, "What Is 'Brain Hacking?'
   Tech Insiders on Why You Should Care," CBS News, April 9,
   2017, https://www.cbsnews.com/news/brain-hacking-tech
   -insiders-60-minutes.

4. Ibid.

5. Ibid.

6. American Psychiatric Association, *Diagnostic and Statistical Manual of Mental Disorders*, 5th ed. (Arlington, Virginia: American Psychiatric Association Publishing, 2013).

7. Tzu Tsun Luk et al., "Short Version of the Smartphone Addiction Scale in Chinese adults: Psychometric Properties, Sociodemographic, and Health Behavioral Correlates," *Journal of Behavioral Addictions* 7, no. 4 (December 1, 2018): 1157–65, https://doi.org/10.1556/2006.7.2018.105.

8. Min Kwon et al., "The Smartphone Addiction Scale: Development and Validation of a Short Version for Adolescents," *PLoS ONE* 8, no. 12 (2013): e83558, https://doi.org/10.1371/journal.pone.0083558.

9. Bill W., *Alcoholics Anonymous* (Mineola, New York: Ixia Press, 2011).

10. Lee Ann Kaskutas, "Alcoholics Anonymous Effectiveness: Faith Meets Science," *Journal of Addictive Diseases* 28, no. 2 (2009): 145–57, https://doi.org/10.1080/10550880902772464.

11. Bill W., *Alcoholics Anonymous*.

Frequently Asked Questions

1. David Hill et al., "Media and Young Minds," *Pediatrics* 138, no. 5 (November 2016): e20162591, https://doi.org/10.1542/peds.2016-2591.

2. Jean Twenge et al., "Age, Period, and Cohort Trends in Mood Disorder Indicators and Suicide Related Outcomes in a Nationally Representative Dataset," *Journal of Abnormal*

Psychology 128, no. 3 (2019): 185–99, https://doi.org/10.1037 /abn0000410.

3. David Ramsey, "Will Blue Light from Electronic Devices Increase My Risk of Macular Degeneration and Blindness?," *Harvard Health Blog*, May 1, 2019, https://www.health .harvard.edu/blog/will-blue-light-from-electronic-devices -increase-my-risk-of-macular-degeneration-and-blindness -2019040816365.

4. "Computer Vision Syndrome," American Optometric Association, https://www.aoa.org/healthy-eyes/eye-and-vision -conditions/computer-vision-syndrome?sso=y.